RECENT BOOKS
BY EDWARD WAGENKNECHT

Nathaniel Hawthorne, Man and Writer
Mark Twain: The Man and His Work
Washington Irving: Moderation Displayed
Edgar Allan Poe: The Man behind the Legend
Chicago
Seven Daughters of the Theater
Harriet Beecher Stowe: The Known and the Unknown
Dickens and the Scandalmongers
The Man Charles Dickens
Henry Wadsworth Longfellow:
    Portrait of an American Humanist
Merely Players
John Greenleaf Whittier: A Portrait in Paradox
The Personality of Chaucer
As Far as Yesterday
William Dean Howells: The Friendly Eye
The Personality of Milton
James Russell Lowell: Portrait of a Many-sided Man
Ambassadors for Christ
The Personality of Shakespeare
Ralph Waldo Emerson: Portrait of a Balanced Soul
The Films of D. W. Griffith, with Anthony Slide
A Pictorial History of New England
Eve and Henry James: Portraits of Women
    and Girls in His Fiction
Fifty Great American Silent Films, 1912–1920,
    with Anthony Slide
Henry David Thoreau: What Manner of Man?
American Profile, 1900–1909
Gamaliel Bradford
The Novels of Henry James

Daughters of the Covenant

Portraits of Six Jewish Women

Edward Wagenknecht

The University of Massachusetts Press   Amherst, 1983

Library of Congress Cataloging in Publication Data
Wagenknecht, Edward, 1900–
Daughters of the covenant.
Bibliography: p.
Includes index.
1. Women, Jewish—United States—Biography.
2. Jews—United States—Biography. 3. Women—United
States—Biography. I. Title.
E184.J5W14 1983   973'.04924022 [B]   83-3562
ISBN 0-87023-396-3

Contents

Preface

THIS BOOK CONTAINS studies of the work and more particularly of the character and personality of the six women considered in it. Why I have chosen this particular half dozen I should find it difficult to say; if my own experience affords a criterion, biographical writers are in large part chosen *by* their subjects, but I can say that I was drawn to them first of all because they interested me as individuals. They do, nevertheless, illustrate various types of Jewish womanhood.

One (Amy Levy) is English, the rest American, and the chronological range is from the birth of Rebecca Gratz in 1781 to the death of Henrietta Szold in 1945. Two (Emma Lazarus and Amy Levy) were writers. Three (Rebecca Gratz, Lillian D. Wald, and Henrietta Szold) were deeply involved with philanthropy. One (Emma Goldman) was a reformer and agitator. One (Rebecca Gratz) was, in spite of her philanthropic and religious activities, essentially a private person. Two (Emma Lazarus and Henrietta Szold) were Zionists; one (Emma Goldman) was anti-Zionist. Only two (Rebecca Gratz and Henrietta Szold) were, in the usual sense of the term, intensely religious Jews; one (Emma Goldman) was an atheist. It was not until I was well along in my work that I realized however that, in one respect at least, my sextette were not at all representative of Jewish womanhood in general. Only one of my subjects (Emma Goldman) was ever married, and her two marriages were not very important in her life, though her numerous extramarital affairs were. As far as we know, Henrietta Szold was the only one of the others who was ever seriously in love.

The arrangement of the six portraits has been determined principally by reference to chronology, slightly modified by considerations of contrast and emphasis. If I had gone by the birth date alone, I should have had to permit Henrietta Szold to precede Amy Levy, but because Amy Levy was dead before 1890 while Henrietta Szold was alive until 1945 and occupied until the end with what are still very much live issues, it seemed better to arrange my subjects primarily by reference to their periods of activity. This consideration alone served adequately to determine the order of the first half of the book but needed to be supplemented by others thereinafter. I will say nothing more about this except that, though I should not be prepared to go to the barricades to defend the thesis that Henrietta Szold is the greatest woman in my book, she still seems to me an eminently suitable figure upon whom to drop the curtain.

Finally, I should like to express my gratitude and appreciation to Professor Robert Tucker, editor of the *Massachusetts Review*, who served as consulting editor for this book. Neither I nor, I am sure, any other writer could ask for a kinder or more sympathetic reader.

E. W.
West Newton, Massachusetts
August 27, 1982

Rebecca Gratz
1781–1869

I

HOMER DID NOT attempt to describe the beauty of Helen directly but confined himself to the effect she had upon others. What else could he have done? Helen was perfect beauty. Was her nose large or small, long or short, wide or pointed? It was none of these; it was just right. It is not the norm but departures from it that furnish good descriptive materials; that is why Dickens's eccentrics are ever so much more memorable than his heroes and heroines.

The Gratzes seem to have been a very handsome family. One admirer said the daughters ought to have been called not Gratzes but Graces, and if we may judge by Thomas Sully's portrait of him, their brother Ben was certainly a very handsome man. Sarah Anne Mordecai calls her Aunt Rachel the outstanding beauty of the family; if this is correct, her portrait by Gilbert Stuart does not do as well by her as Edward Malbone and Sully did by Rebecca. The latter's loveliness did not fail of admirers however, and in character she was something very close to a saint. The outward aspect still lives on canvas (painters have some advantages of which writers are deprived), and her character has been praised by all who knew her or profited by her benefactions, but these things alone do not get us far.

Nevertheless the attempt to make her live again must be made, for if, as I say, Dickens's eccentrics are more memorable than his normal characters, they must have lost their meaning altogether unless he and his readers had kept in mind some kind of norm against which they could be measured. There are not so many people like Rebecca Gratz in the world that we can afford, for our own good, to allow any of them to be forgotten, or at least there are not many the record of whose lives have been preserved of which this can be said; most of them lived so obscurely and so selflessly that the mere fact of their existence survives only in the mind of God. When, a good many years ago, the *New York Times* compiled a list of the ten greatest women in America, the editors carefully explained that they were making their nominations for greatness in terms of the standards by which it is measured in our America. The ten really greatest women in America, the statement continued, have rarely been heard of outside their own homes and have seldom been appreciated there.

Rebecca Gratz was born in Philadelphia on March 4, 1781, and died in that city on August 27, 1869. She was the daughter of Michael and Miriam (Simon) Gratz, the seventh of twelve children, ten of whom survived. The Gratz family had come from Langendorf in Upper Silesia, Michael in 1761, following his brother and business partner Bernard by two years. Mrs. Gratz's father was Joseph Simon, a leading merchant of Lancaster, Pennsylvania, where he had settled about 1740. The merchandising firm of B. and M. Gratz had wide-ranging interests. They were "merchant venturers," involved in fur trading, western land speculation, and coastal shipping. They supported the American Revolution and fitted out privateers; they also advanced supplies for the George Rogers Clark expedition. It has been said that a complete collection of the Gratz family papers between the time of the Seven Years War and the Civil War would involve the whole history of the United States during this period.[1]

Michael Gratz retired in 1798, and his two eldest sons, Simon and Hyman, took over the business. In 1808 his wife died, leaving Rebecca in charge of the household, which at that time included four bachelor brothers and one sister. Michael died in 1811, and in 1826 the firm of S. and H. Gratz failed. The great house on Chestnut Street was sold, and the family removed to much more modest headquarters at No. 2 Boston Row. This was far from being the end of their glory, however. Hyman, who, like his brother Jacob, died in 1857, became president of a life insurance company and of the Pennsylvania Academy of Fine Arts and founder of Gratz College, while Benjamin, the youngest son, who removed to Kentucky and became an associate of Henry Clay and a leader in Kentucky affairs, held a number of offices, being a trustee of Transylvania University, a member of the first governing council of Lexington, one of the incorporators of the Lexington and Ohio Railroad, and much besides. Younger generations of the family have also distinguished themselves in many fields.

When Rachel died in 1823, leaving nine children between the ages of three and sixteen,[2] Rebecca took charge of them and brought them up "by hand," far differently than Mrs. Gargery reared Pip, and after Maria Hoffman died, she looked after her daughter Julia also. The physical, intellectual, and spiritual needs of her charges all received careful attention; she tried to make learning "pleasant and easy" but she did not neglect it; "if we urge a child to learn much, and praise her for it, she becomes vain and superficial, but to require what is learned to be understood and not give her complicated ideas to study which she can not comprehend is much the best plan."[3] I have come across no complaints concerning her dealings with children, but she does complain that the men of the family could be difficult when they were sick; it would be easier, she thought, to take their pain upon herself than to deal with them when they had it!

It would not be correct to leave the impression that Rebecca's early life was devoted to family affairs and that her benevolent activities were confined to her later years, for she helped organize and at the age of twenty became secretary of the Female Association for the Relief of Women and Children in Reduced Circumstances. It is true, however, that as her family cares lessened, she had more time to give to other things. She was a founder and long-time secretary of the nonsectarian Philadelphia Orphan Society, chartered in 1815, and she was important in connection with the beginning of the Female Hebrew Benevolent Society in 1819 and the Jewish Foster Home and Orphan Society in 1855. Nor does this exhaust the list of her efforts toward the amelioration of want.

5

Her services toward the religious education of Jewish children made her an important and historic figure in this field. The first Christian Sunday School in the United States began in 1790, and Rebecca Gratz became interested in extending this movement to Jewish children as early as 1818, when she organized a private Hebrew school in her own home. This effort was short-lived, however, and her real work in this area did not get under way until twenty years later, when the Hebrew Sunday School Society of Philadelphia was founded. This organization endured into the twentieth century and served as a model for similar efforts in other cities. In the beginning Rebecca and Rabbi Isaac Lesser were obliged to make their own textbooks. Rebecca held the presidency until 1864, when she was in her eighties. She herself once described her work with the Jewish Sunday School movement as "the crowning happiness of my life."[4]

II

Thomas Sully painted Rebecca Gratz more than once, and, according to Miriam Biskin, he also tried his hand with words in his notebook:

Never seen a more striking Hebraic face. The easy pose, suggestive of perfect health, the delicately turned neck and shoulders with the firmly poised head and its profusion of dark curling hair, large clear black eyes, the contour of the face, the fine white skin, the expressive mouth and the firmly chiseled nose, with its strength of character, left no doubt as to the race from which she had sprung. Possessed of elegant bearing, a melodiously sympathetic voice, a simple and frank and generous womanliness, there was about Rebecca Gratz all that a princess of Blood Royal would have coveted.

It will be noted that Sully speaks of "perfect health," and we hear little to the contrary aside from the mention of passing indispositions. Once she speaks of both her health and her spirits as being "low," and once, more surprisingly, of having been laid low by feeding too "luxuriously" during the Passover season. In her old age, though swallowing was made difficult for her by a slight paralysis of the throat, she always continued to reply to inquiries concerning health by thanking God that she was well. From Mrs. Mordecai's statement that at the Sunday School, "her majestic figure rose high above all there collected," I should judge that she must have been fairly tall.

She did not believe in borrowing trouble or preparing for it by anticipation ("for when we have experienced much happiness the arrival of crosses teaches us how to bear them"), but she knew that the tenure by which we hold our blessings is at best a frail one, and in her own view she possessed a considerable capacity for irrational worry. Though she was the last person to indulge what her successors would call their "temperament," she was frank to acknowledge that the effects of "dull weather and dyspepsia, stocking darning and ennui" might be "stupefying." Like the rest of the saints, she shows that the human conscience always harries most those who need it least, for her "nightly pillow" was brooded over by the remembrance of each day's deeds, and if she could find any "inconsiderate words and acts" among them, her rest was disturbed. She is said never to have ceased to reproach herself for one act of disobedience when, against her mother's advice, she insisted on wearing mourning for a New York friend, and even in her eighties she prayed to God to "accept my deep felt penitence, for all the sins of commission and omission of duties, of which my conscience accuses me, toward these best of parents," now dead for many years, though it does not appear that anybody can ever have had less to repent of.

III

It is curious that, though neither is inherently improbable, the two things that "everybody knows" about Rebecca Gratz may never have happened. She was a close friend of both Washington Irving, who stayed often enough with the Gratzes so that a room in the Chestnut Street house was called the "Washington Irving Room," and Maria Fenno, who became the second wife of Judge Josiah Ogden Hoffman. It was Matilda, Hoffman's daughter by his previous marriage, who was engaged to Irving and whose death before their contemplated marriage was the great sorrow of his life.

7

According to the legend, Irving sang the praises of Rebecca Gratz to Sir Walter Scott when he visited him at Abbotsford, and it was this which inspired "the Wizard of the North" to create the Jewess Rebecca in *Ivanhoe*, one of the most admired of all his heroines. This story was first told by Gratz Van Renssalaer in 1882, who quoted an alleged letter of Scott's to Irving: "How do you like your Rebecca? Does the Rebecca I have pictured compare well with the pattern given?" This was accepted by W. S. Crockett in *The Scott Originals*, Mrs. Mordecai paraphrases Scott's alleged phrasing in her little book about her aunt, and the quotation has been echoed by many later writers. If its authenticity could be established, we should have an airtight case, but nobody has ever seen such a letter, and it seems highly unlikely that Scott could have written it at a time when the authorship of the Waverley Novels was still a well-guarded secret.[5] Legend adds that when Rebecca Gratz was once asked whether she was the original of the girl in *Ivanhoe*, she replied, "They say so, my dear," but all anybody has ever cited as documentary evidence is that she greatly admired Scott's heroine (and him for having created her) as "such a representation of a good girl as I think human nature can reach." Those readers (and they have been many) who have regretted that Ivanhoe married Rowena instead of Rebecca were already vocal in 1820, but Rebecca Gratz was knowing enough to realize that such an interfaith marriage could not have happened in England in the twelfth century, and she gave Ivanhoe due credit for having fought for Rebecca even though he despised her race. The legend may of course be true despite our inability to prove it, but the only person who ever triumphantly resolved the debate concerning the relative merits of Scott's twin heroines was Kate Douglas Wiggin, who named the enchanting young heroine of *Rebecca of Sunnybrook Farm* Rebecca Rowena Randall!

Oddly enough, this ties in with the other Gratz legend, that Rebecca stifled the great love of her life by refusing to marry Samuel Ewing, son of Dr. John Ewing, a Christian minister and the first provost of the University of Pennsylvania, because of the difference between their faiths. If this is correct, then Rebecca Gratz agreed on one point with Ivanhoe and with Scott's Rebecca also, whom she praises, in the letters from which I have already quoted, for her "beautiful" and "regulated" sensibility, showing "the triumph of faith over human affection." There is more to support this story than the one which involves Scott and Irving, for, unlike his beloved, Ewing did not live out his days in single blessedness, and, according to family tradition, he told his bride-to-be of his love for Rebecca, with whom both she and her children became warm friends. It is further related that when he died, Rebecca visited the house to stay alone with the body for an hour and that when she left she deposited three white roses and her miniature in the casket.[6]

All this is the more interesting in view of both Rebecca's own relations with Gentiles (it would be no exaggeration, I believe, to say that, during her early life at least, she had more Gentile than Jewish friends) and the fact that marriage with a Gentile was by no means unfamiliar to her family. The best-known instance is that of Benjamin, who first married Maria Gist and, after her death, her widowed niece Ann Maria Boswell Shelby, and none of whose descendants was reared in the Jewish faith. Rebecca did not pretend to approve of either marriage, but she took both women to her heart without reservations; not many persons can ever have received such loving letters from a sister-in-law as she wrote to Maria and Ann, and not many human beings can have combined such zeal for their own faith with such respect for that of others as did Rebecca. It was simply that marriage was for her a spiritual as well as a physical relationship, and she could not endure the thought of any shadow of difference in the area of what she regarded as the crowning aspect of human experience between human beings in such a relationship.

IV

Next to nothing seems to have been recorded concerning the education of Rebecca Gratz. Mrs. Mordecai speaks of her having at one time attended a school presided over by a mistress whose Yankee Doodle kind of brother would appear in the schoolroom each day upon the stroke of noon, attired in short knee breeches, shoe buckles, white stockings, and ruffled shirt, say "Good morning" and nothing more, offer his sister a pinch of snuff, and then withdraw. This hardly seems a model educational institution, but presumably whatever education Rebecca received at the schools she may have attended would have been supplemented by private tutors. In any case, she was obviously interested in everything that was supposed to interest cultivated young ladies in her place and time.

Persons who are sensitive to beauty normally respond with warmth to both nature and art. Rebecca loved November, "a thousand times more lovely than May," she calls it, "except that the parting songs of the birds are not so joyful, and the brilliant colors of the forest give one the melancholy thought that their beauty is passing away." In another passage, however, she is ecstatic about spring. She had always loved it, she says, but now, as she grows older, it seems lovelier than ever: "nature is our first and last love, for we outgrow taste for every pleasure less enduring and less pure." Perhaps, like many of us, she would have had difficulty deciding between the two seasons. She loved those "good angels," the flowers, always, "a creation of pure benevolence with which God has ornamented the earth, to make it more lovely and to gladden the heart of those who dwell on it." When, in the midst of the Civil War, they spring up in all their beauty, the earth itself seems to her to be reproaching "the wickedness of man in this unholy strife, and women too! more monstrous still, who step out of the sphere God designed them to fill in such times of trouble."

Rebecca did not live in a scientific age, and her interest in nature did not carry over into science, but "Horace's silk worms" and a collection of shells sent to her from the West Indies did make her ashamed of her ignorance "on the most interesting of all studies." Nevertheless, after reading and hearing Combe and Spurzheim, she showed more interest in phrenology than in anything that would be considered authentic science today. It might be useful, she thought, not only in choosing professions for boys, "when the whole map of the mind is drawn in legible marks on the skull" but also in repressing "evil propensities" and developing good ones.

I find little about music or the plastic arts. She notes the coming of Jenny Lind to Philadelphia under the sponsorship of P. T. Barnum but resents the selling of tickets by auction at exorbitant prices and does not plan to go. It is clear, however, that she attended the theater with reasonable frequency, where her great enthusiasm was for her friend Fanny Kemble, whose Shakespeare readings she thought outstanding. Fanny Kemble seemed to her "to understand every character in the whole play and give appropriate tones to every speaker, exhibit every passion, varying her voice and manner to the very cadence of the scene she reads of." Indeed she was so good that her admirer was not sure she could ever be satisfied by any regular performance by other actors again, a view in which she was in entire accord with Longfellow, both being in flat disagreement with Dickens, himself no mean platform artist, who considered Mrs. Kemble's readings phenomenally bad.

She was more concerned with literature than any other art. I am surprised to have found no references to foreign languages beyond one to studying Hebrew in 1818. She quotes from many writers in her letters, and her niece says she often repeated "Universal Prayer," "Edwin and Angelina," and something from *The Lady of the Lake*, not always remembering the source of her quotation. She was fond of Cowper, and she seems to have had a weakness for Young, who encouraged her to remember that man's hold upon happiness was "as frail, as attenuated as a spider's thread." But judging by the frequency with which she quotes from him in her letters, she would seem to have known Shakespeare better than any other writer; as long as language endures, she thought, he "will commune with the human heart, and will reach out a fellowship, which no distance of time can change." Despite her interest in contemporary Romantics, however, she insisted upon her niece's also reading Milton and Pope, "to chastise her taste and give her other standards of excellence."

She notes the appearance of successive works by popular literati on both sides of the Atlantic, including Irving, Scott, Cooper, James K. Paulding, John Pendleton Kennedy, and Catharine Sedgwick, some of whom were her friends. Like

Irving and Miss Sedgwick, she showed interest in the pathetic and ill-starred Davidson sisters–Lucretia Maria and Margaret Miller.[7] She knew that the flowering of American literature was something yet to come, but she believed it surely would.

I have observed only one reference to Dickens in the Philipson *Letters*, and it is couched in general terms. Rebecca knew Carlyle at least by *Sartor Resartus*. She defends Bulwer-Lytton's *Eugene Aram* as at least less dangerous than some of his other books because the hero's crime is followed by such "signal punishment," but when Bulwer's terrible wife publishes a novel reputed to be based upon their married life, she reads the "stupid immoral thing" because she had always thought so badly of him that she hoped the book would tend to put down "the fashion of admiring the poison distilled from" his "profligate pen," and when Mary Shelley brings out *The Last Man*, she finds it "worth more than her other book" (she does not say which one) but still thinks it far from inculcating "good principles." She felt much safer with Hannah More and Maria Edgeworth, and she liked Harriet Martineau much when she came to the United States ("such a woman as one rarely meets, and cannot fail to admire"), though she cannot possibly have approved of her views on the subject of religion, if she knew what they were.

Rebecca Gratz clearly enjoyed reading novels, especially historical novels, though she also shared in the general tendency of her time to regard the reading of fiction as a trifling amusement, defensible on the ground that it was better than idleness or took the place of something worse. Her own reading, however, was not confined to fiction. She speaks of reading, or at least of reading some part of Jared Sparks's biography of Washington, she was familiar with the letters of Madame de Sévigné and Lady Mary Wortley Montagu, and she attended Henry N. Hudson's lectures on Shakespeare. Occasionally she mentions Jewish writers like Grace Aguilar and Moses Mendelssohn, but for some reason she seems to have believed that the Cabala was the name of a book instead of a term indicating Jewish mystical lore.[8] Her comments on her reading seldom go into detail; perhaps those on Prescott's *Ferdinand and Isabella* are the most interesting, and here she had a built-in interest from being Jewish.

I must confess I turn with disgust from the intolerance and superstition of the age and can scarcely agree with the historian in his praise of Isabella's benevolence and piety when the stake and the gibbet were continually reeking with the blood of Jews and heretics—it is a bad argument for one in so responsible a position as the Queen that she was under the dominion of her priests—however great allowance must be made for the spirit of the age she lived in, and she was the admiration and wonder of her day.

When "institutions founded under the auspices of religion" became "first the tools and then the victims of fiery zeal and superstition," Rebecca was driven to the conclusion that "we must turn to individual exceptions if we would be reconciled to our own species," and she could only regret that Isabella was not such an exception. There is one reference to her intending to read *The Conquest of Mexico*, but I do not know whether she carried out her intention.

V

Yet I think she was always more interested in direct contact with human beings than in their expression of themselves in art. To be sure, she did better with men and women as individuals than in the mass. She had some but hardly an overwhelming or deeply penetrating interest in public affairs; she was in no respect a "strong-minded woman." She had opinions upon a variety of subjects, however, and expressed them frankly. She considered imprisonment for debt the most unreasonable and unjust of all laws, thought Louis Kossuth on his American tour a humbug, and feared the development of trade unionism with what she saw as its policy of high wages or no work. She disliked Andrew Jackson but not so much as she admired Henry Clay, who became an intimate friend of her brother Ben and into whose family Ben's youngest daughter married. As long as he was in the running, she passionately backed Clay's presidential aspirations and looked forward to going to Washington for his inauguration, but both he and she died with this hope unfulfilled.[9]

We of the twentieth century have acquired horrors with which Rebecca Gratz was blessedly unfamiliar, but she had two to cope with which no longer concern us: cholera and dueling. Somebody she knew was nearly always fearing or fleeing from the first or dying of the second. There is no doubt whatever as to how she felt about the "detested" and "barbarous" practice of dueling; to her way of thinking those who engaged in it were murderers who had committed an unpardonable sin. In 1849 she was particularly moved by the duel in which both Cassius Clay and his antagonist perished, and she thought that even if these "misguided men" had no scruples against killing or being killed themselves, at least "human affections" might "have saved them from involving their unhappy wives in such desolation and ruin!" Much earlier than this she had written, "I wish we were a less barbarous people and could count among us heroes who would not stain their hands with human blood, unless in the field of battle for their country's honor and safety."

But, as this last quotation shows, she was less radical or penetrating on wholesale than retail murder. Nevertheless, all her feelings were against both. She found little to choose between the cruelties perpetrated by the Indians in warfare and those employed by their white opponents against them, and when she is told that General Jackson is protecting our frontiers against the red men, Miriam Biskin has her inquiring who will protect the red men against him. The Gratzes were up to their necks in the War of 1812. The family had three men in service (Rebecca prayed to the "God of battles" to protect them) and the firm engaged in manufacturing gunpowder from saltpeter sent up from Mammoth Cave, but she thought an armistice would bring more honor to the country than all the laurels her heroes could gather. Like most intelligent Northerners, she found more sorrow and disgust than heroism in the Mexican War. "When we were obliged to fight for our liberty and rights there was motive and glory in the strife but to invade a country and slaughter its inhabitants, to fight for boundary or political supremacy, is altogether against my principles and feelings and I shall be most happy when it is over."

The Civil War naturally was a more difficult matter. As

early as 1832 she feared that the Southern nullifiers would break up the Union and set Americans to killing each other, and in 1845 she disapproved of Cassius Clay's abolitionism in Kentucky, seeing it as sure to cause trouble and more likely to worsen the condition of the blacks than improve it. According to David Philipson, Ben, the only Gratz who lived in that state, owned slaves but freed them when the fighting began. Miriam Biskin quotes Rebecca as saying that "the master is as enslaved as the slave; he is so dependent that he is no more free than his chattel," a perspicacious observation. Rebecca had relatives in both armies. The Unionist Cary, Ben's son, died at Willow's Creek, Missouri, just as the conflict was getting under way, but his stepson became a Confederate general. Rebecca prayed for his personal safety but not for the triumph of his cause. She was a warm partisan of General McClellan, whom she saw as the faithful protector of his men while others were allowing theirs to suffer unnecessary hardships, and she profoundly mistrusted England and English intentions toward the Union.

VI

It must not be forgotten, however, that Rebecca Gratz was always a private woman, and, as I have already suggested, she is most impressive in her contacts with individual human beings. Though the Gratzes lived an active social life, we find Rebecca writing Maria Hoffman as early as 1807 that though she attends teas or balls three or four evenings a week, she no longer enjoys such things as she did when she was younger. When you live as long as she did in so large a family with so wide a circle of friends, you are bound to encounter death with melancholy frequency, but Rebecca was only forty when she wrote that parties had become " 'stale, flat and unprofitable' " to her because her "companions of former days" had "either passed away or . . . lost their interest in my heart and the idea has so much of melancholy in it to me that a ball-room seems more like a memorial of lost pleasures than an incitement to new ones."

With her brother Hyman, who was noted for his elegance, and sometimes attended by other brothers and nieces, she seems often to have attended Saratoga Springs and other fashionable spas, though even there she complains that both young and old are " 'converting pleasure into toil and fancying toil a pleasure.' " She seems to have done little traveling and hardly any for traveling's sake. In 1848 she wrote Ann Gratz that she had been born too early to be fashionable; in 1849 she complains that railroad travel sacrifices much in the way of picturesqueness; and in 1852 she is worried about steamboat accidents and the indifference of those who manage them to public safety.

Her seriousness, her moderation, and her good sense are as evident in her social life as in any other aspect. She loved people and craved contact with them, judging no effort she could make for the comfort of relatives and friends and for those who needed help too great. She knew that it was sometimes easier to express one's feelings on paper than by word of mouth, yet she could not accept letters as a really satisfying substitute for personal contact, for she craved the pleasure of looking into the eyes of those she loved and "reading that untranslatable language of the soul," but she knew too that the conditions necessary to achieve that kind of contact were generally far from ideal at balls and teas.

Only she was never fanatical about any of this. She knew that complete frankness between human beings is neither possible nor humane, and she had no patience with those whose pride in their candor took the form of lacerating the feelings of others by describing their shortcomings "for their own good," as the saying is, or repeating everything they had heard to their discredit, and this is typical of her whole attitude toward social relations. She was much too pretty herself to share the mistrust of beauty often professed by those who have it not: "I have heard many speak of the perils of beauty, who spoke very wisely, but I doubted the sincerity of their hearts, if they would not still say that they would encounter the peril to possess the gift." Boarding schools she mistrusted as "too much an epitome of fashionable life to be the safest place for regulating the taste and feelings of a girl approaching womanhood," but she had a woman's interest in shops, which she enjoyed even if she did not wish to purchase, and in pretty clothes, and she wished every girl to have the happiest girlhood possible as the best preparation for a useful mature life. Clothes were important because she believed that many people both felt better and acted better when they were well dressed. Dancing too had its place, even with boys. "I am much pleased at the figures our boys make in the ball room–grace is a passport to favor, and by no means to be neglected. . . . Why should we not put all innocent appliances in our children's power to enjoy– pleasure is but short lived, and we must not let the proper season pass–you can mix graver studies for use, but there is still time for dancing and mirth." But she always remembered that good manners have value only as the index to an inner spiritual grace. Indeed beauty itself was "independent of features in a great degree"; a plain face with a kind heart, a good temper, and gentle speech was worth more than beautiful features alone with these things absent.

Rebecca's natural attitude toward human beings was warm and friendly. She knew that misfortune brings people closer together and felt that she gained more insight during a week's visit to a troubled neighbor's nursery than through the whole three years of their previous acquaintance. She was grateful too for the sympathy shown by others to her own family when their financial difficulties came upon them. She resented affectation, aggression, and assumptions of superiority, as with a Mrs. Caldwell, who considered herself ordained to set the fashion for those around her and supply them with "an endless variety from her own fertile genius," and a Mrs. Russel, an enthusiast for "everything Savage," who much desired to paint an Indian but could not find one handsome enough to suit her. She was also quite unimpressed by a clergyman who told his congregation that he had left a dead child in order to bring them the sacrament; if he had felt his loss as he should, she thought, he would have either stayed at home or performed his clerical duties without boasting. She judges one rabbi a good man but neither a learned man nor a very sensible one and rates another ugly and awkward though sensible and pious, and she bluntly labels one couple criminals and vipers and wishes there were some way to save their children from being reared by them.

She did not unduly idealize human beings, for she knew that in any race or nation or crisis it is not safe to count on more than a minority taking the intelligent, enlightened, humane, and unselfish view, and she knew too that these people alone make it possible to continue to believe in human nature. (Did she remember, one wonders, what Isaiah said about the remnant?) Nevertheless, it was not her way to reject the whole because of the weakness of a part. In her eyes the actress and dramatist, Anna Cora Ogden Mowatt, the author of *Fashion*, was "decidedly Theatrical" and a lover of notoriety, but she still valued her "noble traits of character and strong affections." She was pleased too when John Randolph's letters revealed elements of tenderness in his character of whose existence she had not previously been aware and was glad to be able to discount his eccentricities as aberrations of mind, and she adds charitably that he might have been very different with a good wife, since, whatever their own opinion of the matter may be, "the lords of creation" are the most helpless of all beings when they have to look after themselves. As long as she could, she tried to believe the best of people, not the worst; this is nowhere better shown than in her attitude toward a "singular" but unfortunate woman from Missouri, a divorcée whose manners left much to be desired but whom she commended to her brother Ben without really knowing very much about her. Ben, she knew, would not choose her as a companion for his wife; nevertheless she deserved protection as "a stranger in the land, oppressed, and slandered, cast off by her husband for no crime and only meaning to prosecute her rights so far as to enable her to live reputably in her own country."

VII

Rebecca Gratz lived for her family, for her religion, and to help others, and for her there was no conflict between these ends, for she thought of religion in terms of loving service toward God's children. Mrs. Mordecai writes: "Nothing could be lovelier than her every day life, which commenced every morning with prayers and thanks to the Creator for support and for protecting her through the night, and ended with renewed thanks for the blessings bestowed during the day, while the record of every day's life was a lesson to everyone around her, fulfilling every duty with patience, kindness, humility and love."

Although the Gratzes were Ashkenazic Jews, the only synagogue available to them in Philadelphia was orthodox and Sephardic, and I have no doubt that Rebecca fulfilled all the requirements of orthodox Jewry faithfully and uncomplainingly. There was no bigotry in her and no cant; neither was her religious emphasis otherworldly. The "recorded self abasement of sanctified persons" did not appeal to her, and though she well knew that all human beings must be on guard continually against temptation, she still felt that "to sink into the slough of despondency because we are placed a little lower than the angels was an affront to the Divine order," nor had she any sympathy with those moralists who called this world "by such hard names that one would think God had withdrawn his favor from the beautiful planet he created in love and bestowed all his treasures on another State."

Many of her utterances on religious matters seem indistinguishable from those of orthodox Christians in her time. She professes "implicit faith in Scripture," and she seems to have had no shadow of doubt concerning human immortality. Her late friend Mrs. Cohen, she feels, was as well prepared to meet death as any human being can be, and when children die, she always comforts their parents with the thought that they will know them again on another plane of being. Certainly she was no intellectual in matters of religion; indeed there are times when she seems naive. She attributes to God Himself a direct and minute control over the lives of all. When the Gratz house escapes destruction from a nearby fire, she carefully states that she does not attribute this to chance, and changes in the weather are ascribed to the decrees of providence, so that in the long run everything is ordered for the best. The most untimely deaths in the family are attributed to God's will, and it is the duty of the bereaved to submit, though they may not understand. She seems to extend this belief even to death in battle; apparently it did not occur to her that if God were responsible for such death, He must have willed the battle also, which would be a faith worse than atheism.

The most remarkable thing about her religious attitude is the way she was able to combine her own religious zeal with entire respect for the religious beliefs of others. She was friendly with the Unitarian Reverend William Henry Furness, who was the father of the great editor of the New Variorum Shakespeare, Horace Howard Furness, and often went to hear him preach. Furness used to tease her. Their religious beliefs were not very far apart, he told her, yet they were not identical; they ought therefore to be enemies, to which she replied that she "claimed the privilege of not being inimical to any man's religion, yet being firmly attached to my own," and nobody who ever lived could have been better qualified to say this. "The sublime, beneficent holy Spirit, to which all forms are but the outward costumes in which different nations choose to dress it is still the same, and all who lift their souls on high in Adoration may walk the earth in charity with one another."

Rebecca met Christian bigotry in connection with the Furnesses themselves when the nonsectarian orphan asylum with which she was connected refused to allow Mrs. Furness to take an orphan girl into her home because she was a Unitarian. Would you refuse me, asked Rebecca, because I am a Jew? No, was the reply, because Jews do not proselytize. She was not pleased, but she cannot have been much better satisfied when in 1841 she petitioned the Congregation Mikveh Israel to allow Mary Gratz, daughter of her brother Simon and his non-Jewish wife, to be buried in their cemetery, and the request was denied. We have already seen how cordially she received both of Ben's Gentile wives into the family. She spelled it out nobly in a letter to him: "I love your dear Maria, and admire the forbearance which leaves unmolested the religious opinions she knows are sacred in your estimation. May you both continue to worship according to the dictates of your conscience and your orisons be equally acceptable at the throne of Grace." But the most touching example of her generous spirit came early in her life when her dying grandfather Joseph Simon asked her whether there was anything he could do for her before he died and she replied, "Forgive Aunt Shinah, grandfather–please." Simon's daughter had married Dr. Nicholas Schuyler in defiance of her father's wishes, and he had never seen her since, but he granted Rebecca's plea and reconciliation ensued.

I began this discussion by enlarging upon the difficulties involved in describing perfection, and I hope I have not therefore produced an essay in hagiography. Rebecca Gratz was a human being with the limitations of humanity. In the following pages we shall be concerned with some women who possessed gifts that she was denied, a more penetrating intelligence or a deeper insight into certain human problems, but we shall encounter no better or more loving human being nor one more worthy to be loved. Though she obviously possessed considerable executive ability, Rebecca Gratz functioned largely in woman's traditional sphere in a fashion that some of her posterity would now describe as "old fashioned." But, as Chesterton once reminded us, our time, like hers, is a time, and not the Day of Judgment, and it is not necessary to take sides between her and them in order to realize that we may well be better men and women for having known her, and that if we are not, the fault belongs to us alone.

Emma Lazarus

1849–1887

I

EMMA LAZARUS WAS a pioneer Zionist and one of the very first writers to strike an authentically Jewish note in American literature, but most readers today merely think of her as the only poet who has ever had the honor of having her verses engraved upon the pedestal of the Statue of Liberty:

> "Give me your tired, your poor,
> Your huddled masses yearning to breathe free,
> The wretched refuse of your teeming shore.
> Send these, the homeless, tempest-tost to me,
> I lift my lamp beside the golden door!"

In her time she was known for much more. Bryant thought the verses in her first book, *Poems and Translations Written Between the Ages of Fourteen and Sixteen*, better than any others he had seen by a girl of her age; when she sent Turgenev her only novel, *Alide*, he professed himself proud of her approbation and assured her that she was no longer a pupil but well on her way to mastery;[1] British critics thought her "Admetus" superior to Browning's *Belaustion's Adventure* and her "Tannhäuser" better than "The Hill of Venus" by William Morris. Her American admirers included John Greenleaf Whittier, Thomas Wentworth Higginson, Charles Dudley Warner, Edward Eggleston, H. H. Boyesen, John Burroughs, E. L. Godkin, E. C. Stedman, William and Henry James, John Hay, and Henry George, and when she went to England, she was welcomed by Robert Browning, William Morris, Edmund Gosse, Austin Dobson, Thomas Henry Huxley, and Sir Edward Burne-Jones.

James Russell Lowell, to be sure, refused to print her poems in the *North American Review*, thinking that she needed to do more work on them (he partly atoned for this later when he told her he liked "The New Colossus" better than the Statue of Liberty itself), and Howells rejected "Admetus" when Emerson sent it to the *Atlantic*, thinking it too derivative, a view with which Emerson did not agree. But Emerson himself presents a problem. Though he found the classical influence too strong in her early work and urged her not to neglect "the despised Present," he practically made a protégée of her and then nearly broke her heart by excluding her from his immense poetic anthology, *Parnassus*, which included the work of many less gifted poets than she.[2] We do not know whether he replied to the letter of protest and inquiry she wrote him, but he did invite her to Concord, where she made friends with Mrs. Emerson and Ellen, was not attracted by Bronson Alcott, and established fairly close relations with Ellery Channing, though she described him as "a gnarled and twisted shrub—a pathetic, impossible creature." After Emerson's death, she summed up her impressions of him with dignity in the *Century Magazine*.[3]

Emma Lazarus was born in New York City on July 22, 1849, the daughter of Moses Lazarus, a Sephardic Jew and wealthy sugar refiner, and his wife, Esther Nathan, who was of Ashkenazic stock. Both parents came from families of assured position and some distinction which had been in this country since before the Revolution. The girl grew up in a household which ultimately embraced seven living children, all but one of them girls, of whom she was the fourth. The death of her mother in 1874 probably made her more dependent upon her father, who had retired from business at fifty-two, nine years before. He lived until 1885, four years before her own death.

She was educated at home by tutors and began writing and translating poetry very early. Her indulgent father had her first collection privately printed in 1866; the next year it was published by Hurd and Houghton, who, in 1871, followed it with the considerably more mature *Admetus and Other Poems*. Her only novel, *Alide*, which is based on

Goethe's own account of his youthful affair with Fredricka Brion, followed in 1874, and *The Spagnoletto*, a lurid Renaissance tragedy or melodrama about José (or Juseppe) Ribera, a sixteenth-seventeenth-century Neapolitan painter, was privately printed in 1876. Just before the final curtain, Ribera kills himself in front of his daughter, thinking this the most effective way to punish her for having allowed herself to be seduced by Don John of Austria. This climax is more horrifying than effective, and Emma herself decided that the play was unactable, but it is included in the first volume of her collected poems. The next year she made, from German texts, her first translations from the Jewish poets of mediaeval Spain, and in 1881 she published her translation of *Poems and Ballads of Heinrich Heine*.

She became a prolific contributor to both Hebrew and general American magazines (*Lippincott's*, the *Critic*, and the *Century* were particularly hospitable to her), and in 1882 she published her *Songs of a Semite*, which includes her other tragedy, *The Dance to Death*, the story of a fourteenth-century pogrom that had been fired by the same kind of insane accusations against Jews as were being revived in eastern Europe in her own time. If *The Dance to Death* is not quite an acting drama either, it is certainly much more powerful to read than *The Spagnoletto*. "An Epistle to the Hebrews" was serialized in the *American Hebrew* in 1882–83 but did not appear as a book during the author's lifetime. By now she was deep in propaganda and relief activities occasioned by the plight of eastern European Jews pouring into this country after the persecutions following the assassination of Czar Alexander II. She made two trips to England and the Continent, in 1883 and 1885, but she was fatally ill of cancer, and in 1887 she returned home to die in New York at the cruelly early age of thirty-eight. Her death drew extensive press coverage, and perhaps George W. Cable's valedictory was the most adequate: "She was the worthy daughter of a race to which the Christian world owes a larger debt of gratitude incurred from the days of Abraham until now, and from which it should ask more forgiveness than to and from any other people that ever trod the earth."

II

Her photographs show a long, slender face, with fine, rather deep-set eyes, comparatively large nose and ears, finely modeled mouth and chin, and dark hair braided firmly around her head. One writer speaks of her face as a "forest densely populated with thought," and she is said to have been capable of quick changes of expression, passing at a bound from severity to tenderness. Stedman found her "thoroughly feminine and a mistress of the social art and charm." She was an ornament of the Richard Watson Gilders's salon, and Rose Hawthorne Lathrop says she conversed with celebrities with ease. John Burroughs told her frankly that he liked her and wanted to see more of her, at the same time reproving her for thinking too meanly of herself, and she enjoyed a warm friendship with the great Italian actor Salvini. No doubt it would have been more dignified not to bare her heart to Emerson after he had cut her to the quick by leaving her out of *Parnassus*, but her protest was expressed with dignity and without self-vaunting; speaking generally, I should say that her letters to the Emersons and other literary folk whom she had approached or who had taken an interest in her are frank, affectionate, and free from fawning, equally compounded of modesty and self-respect.

In the biographical memoir prefaced to her collected poems, her sister Josephine accents her modesty: "She was a born singer; poetry was her natural language, and to write was less effort than to speak, for she was a shy, sensitive child, with strange reserves and reticences, not easily putting herself *en rapport* with those around her. Books were her world from her earliest years; in them she literally lost and found herself." Indeed "her unwillingness to assert herself or to claim any prerogative" went beyond modesty to morbidness, and she was even inclined to resent any reference to her work.

When Stedman lent her the poems of Mrs. James T. Fields, she wrote that "what you say about their resemblance to my own work confirms me more than ever in the opinion I have long held of my verses—that they are not of the slightest value or importance to the world." Mrs. Fields's poems seemed to her "very sweet, graceful and delicate," but there was nothing in them "to stir, to awaken, to teach, or to suggest, nothing that the world could not equally well do without."[4] In a more intimate vein, she wrote Ellen Emerson that she believed herself more dependent upon expressions of friendship and confidence from those she loved than most persons are, "not from any lack of confidence in their kindness or loyalty" but because of her own "painful distrust" of her capacity to inspire affection. Obviously she habitually kept her own defenses up, for, as she wrote Emerson himself, she found "a certain egotism in . . . holding up the glass to one's heart and mind. I think after all, modesty and the concealing of one's fault imply at least contrition and a desire to be better, but declaring them openly requires a degree of boldness and shamefacedness which tends to intensify them." Nor did she believe that those who attempted to make a clean breast of things often achieved it; some concealment was nearly always practiced, and when the meanest and most contemptible faults were confessed, they were often so presented as almost to reconcile their possessor to them.

She herself judged that her natural inclination tended too much in the direction of retirement and she was consistent to the end in her refusal to participate in public speaking, though she sometimes agreed to write a lecture which somebody else could read for her. For all that, she was no shrinking violet; had she been, she could never have nerved herself to take the public stands she did during her later years. Mary Cohen quotes "one who was very closely related to her" as having said that "she was always on fire about something." In one letter to Ellen Emerson she reproaches herself for a habitual bluntness of expression, and Ellen herself thought her "a pleasant–if somewhat intense–companion." Even in the tribute to her published in the *Critic* after her death, "her playful, though sometimes sardonic wit" is spoken of.

She did not care to be misrepresented. When she heard that the *American Hebrew* had adopted what she considered an undignified way of advertising her writings, she protested with spirit, and when its editor Philip Cowen tried to brush away her protest about misprints in one of her articles as unimportant, she would have none of it. In one case she had been made "guilty of a grammatical blunder," while in another the omission of a word had deprived her sentence of meaning, and to her such things were not trifling. She added notes to her poems to make it clear that "Admetus" had been written before "The Love of Alcestis," and "Tann-häuser" before "The Hill of Venus," and that therefore she was not indebted to the work of other writers. Even her last, grueling illness did not, it seems, quench her spirit, since her sister writes that clear to the end, though wasted physically to a shadow, "she talked about art, poetry, the scenes of travel, of which her brain was full, and the phases of her own condition, with an eloquence for which even those who knew her best were quite unprepared."

All this seems far removed from the graveyard atmosphere of her first book. A girl in her teens, she was fond of identifying herself with elderly persons looking back over a disappointing life, and there is unintended humor in such poems as "On a Lock of My Mother's Hair":

> In looking o'er the souvenirs
> Of days when I was young,
> I found a lock of silver hair
> The tokens dear among.

As absurdly as the young James Russell Lowell, she had *"ge-lebt und geliebt"*:

> Yes, I have lived through many weary years
> Of suffering, and grief, and endless pain,
> And little joy, and bitter, bitter years;
> And all my darkened life, has been in vain,
> For what is left me in my old age now?
> These locks of snow.

In the stanza following this one she adds that she had "loved, and madly loved, and long, / With all the passion of a woman's longing" and that now, in her old age, she has been left with a broken heart. "Beginning and End" mourns the death of a lover; "A Cradle and a Grave" is a lament for a dead baby; "The Broken Toy" is written from the point of view of a little boy who had been badly treated by "a lovely maiden" who was obviously spoiling for a whipping which should have left her unable to sit down; in "Rest at Last" peace comes only as we "float down the stream of Death." It is hard to tell how much of this is temperamental and how much is due to the literary fashion of the day, but I think everybody would agree that humor is not a prominent element in either her life or her work.

III

Primarily she was a lady of letters, but what else did she care for? Obviously no beauty-loving temperament, above all that of a nineteenth-century poet, could be indifferent to nature. Emma Lazarus once wrote Emerson that, except for Thoreau and Whitman, she had even dismissed books for the time being in favor of the world lying around her. "Of all seasons, Autumn is the one whose approach I love best to watch. I have seen with delight the bronzing trees of the woods, and the trembling poplars sprinkling their silver with gold, and the later flowers and fruits blooming and ripening."

She also had a special feeling for the sea (her early summers were spent near it at Newport and elsewhere), and some of her sea poems have erotic implications. Her last day on shipboard during her first trip to England was a "vision of beauty from morning till night–the sea like a mirror and the sky dazzling with light." But she did not need spectacular or unusual aspects of nature to delight her. So she can write in "Phantasies":

> The ceaseless whirr of crickets fills the ear
> From underneath each hedge and bush and tree,
> Deep in the dew-drenched grasses everywhere.
>
> The simple sound dispels the fantasy
> Of gloom and terror gathering round the mind.
> It seems a pleasant thing to breathe, to be,
>
> To hear the many-voiced, soft summer wind
> Lisp through the dark thick leafage overhead—
> To see the rosy half-moon soar behind

The black slim-branching elms. Sad thoughts have fled,
Trouble and doubt, and now strange reveries
And odd caprices fill us in their stead.

When, during her final, ultimately fatal illness, she believed
at one time that her disease had left her, she wrote with un-
conscious pathos, "There is no such cure for pessimism as a
severe illness. The simplest pleasures become enough–to
breathe the air and see the sun."

When she got to England, the appeal of natural beauty became entangled for her with literary associations that had
sweetened all her life; though she was not of English extrac-
tion, no American of her time felt the appeal of what Hawthorne called "our old home" more strongly. "To American
eyes," she wrote, "no bit of rural England can be devoid of
interest and charm"; to her "the most ordinary objects"
seemed "under a spell," as if "to bewitch us back into the
dream-world of a previous existence." In Rome the association was less with literature than with art. "I am wild with
the excitement of this tremendous place," she wrote. "It is
all heart-breaking." The almond trees were in bloom, the
grass was covered with violets, and "oh! the divine, the ce-
lestial, the unheard-of beauty of it all!" One of her biogra-
phers even has her buying paints and canvas toward the end
of her life. Greek sculpture enraptured her also, "wiping out
all other places and impressions, and opening a whole new
world of sensations." Whether or not she attempted painting, there can be no question that she began a serious study
of Rembrandt preparatory to writing "a critical analysis" of
his "genius and personality" which her cruel malady did not
permit her to write. But her visit to Paris did produce the fine
sonnet about the Venus de Milo which ties up with her life-
long interest in Heine and practically identifies her with him.

Down the long hall she glistens like a star,
The foam-born mother of Love, transfixed in stone,
Yet none the less immortal, breathing on.
Time's brutal hand hath maimed but could not mar.
When first the enthralled enchantress from afar
Dazzled mine eyes, I saw her not alone,
Serenely poised on her world-worshipped throne,

As when she guided once her dove-drawn car,—
But at her feet a pale, death-stricken Jew,
Her life adorer, sobbed farewell to love.
Here *Heine* wept! Here still he weeps anew,
Nor ever shall his shadow lift or move,
While mourns one ardent heart, one poet-brain,
For vanished Hellas and Hebraic pain.

A serious interest in painting and sculpture was a late development in Emma's life, but music had been a passion
from the beginning and became more important for her
poetry than the plastic arts ever did. Her Tannhäuser, deprived of his lyre, tells the shepherd boy that

> Whoso hath
> The art to make this speak is raised thereby
> Above all loneliness or grief or fear.

She called Bach, Beethoven, and Handel the supreme composers, but apparently the Romantics better fired her muse,
for she wrote four sonnets to Chopin, and the elaborate
"Phantasies" and "Symphonic Studies," to say nothing of
the uncollected "Scenes in the Wood,"[5] derive from Schumann, though it must be admitted that both Shakespeare
and Botticelli are more obviously present in "Symphonic
Studies."

In the theater her great admiration was for Tommaso Salvini, who became her friend. She did not write much about
the theater, but her two articles about Salvini and the one
about the German actor Ludwig Barnay[6] are enough to
prove that she would have made an excellent drama critic.
She had no patience with the notion that criticism is primarily fault-finding, and she did not pigeonhole artists in any
line of endeavor, but she knew how to describe acting in sufficient detail so that her reader could share her experience,
and her enthusiasm matched her discrimination.

One wonders whether there were any emotional experiences in her life that were not filtered through art. Critics
who believe that all literature is autobiographical have been
tempted to interpret the sequence of lyric poems she called
"Epochs" as indicating that the poet herself had "loved and
lost." This may be so, but we have no corroborative evi-

dence. She was friendly with Thomas Wren Ward, a member of the Emerson circle, and she was obviously, for a time at least, fond of her cousin Washington Nathan, to whom she dedicated "Lohengrin," but that is all we know.

Freud-oriented critics have consequently been led to speculate about the possibility of a "father fixation" in Emma Lazarus and to see the close connection between father and daughter in her two plays as reflecting the writer's own life. It is interesting that in her article on Salvini's Lear, she should have expressed the unusual point of view that Lear's wrath against Cordelia in the opening scene is not, under the circumstances posited, exaggerated. There can be no question that the Lazaruses were a very closely and warmly attached family. Thomas Wentworth Higginson has recorded finding the children almost in despair upon one occasion because their father had to leave home on business for a single night, but John Burroughs thought that what Emma told him of her relations with her father indicated that their association had been exactly what that of father and daughter ought to be.

In Emma Lazarus's novel, *Alide*, Goethe's defection from the heroine is foreshadowed in his comments on *Hamlet*; the prince, he thought, had once sincerely loved Ophelia but had simply outgrown her. Dan Vogel oversimplifies, however, when he sees the author consequently championing the freedom required by the artistic temperament. Her Goethe is no seducer (neither is Alide, in the vulgar sense of the term, seduced); the necessity laid upon him to grow affects the man as much as the artist, and the outcome of the affair would surely have been the same had he never written a line. He and Alide would simply have been hopelessly mismated, and it is she who, perceiving this, makes the break, though it nearly kills her to do it. "Is it not better to part at the beginning of the roads, before they diverge too widely?"

There are fleshly references in "Orpheus" and "Tann-häuser" and "Symphonic Studies." Desire is well expressed in "Spring Longing":

> Swift the liquid golden flame
> Through my frame

Sets my throbbing veins afire.
Bright, alluring dreams arise,
  Brim mine eyes
With the tears of strong desire.

In the fantastic "August Moon" we encounter the ghosts of

maids who died unwed,
And they quit their gloomy bed,
Hungry still for human pleasure,
Here to trip a moonlit measure.

And in "Autumn Sadness" nature itself is presented in erotic
terms:

Such impassioned silence fills
  All the hills
Burning with unflickering fire—
Such a blood-red splendor stains
  The leaves' veins,
Life seems one fulfilled desire.

The most erotic poem Emma Lazarus ever wrote, however, is the Petrarchan sonnet "Assurance," which she never
published and which has been printed only in Dan Vogel's
book about her. Since this expresses love for a woman, not a
man, Arthur Zeiger interpreted it in an unpublished disser-
tation as a lesbian fantasy, but Vogel is surely correct in rejecting this view as nonsense. Women, both poets and novelists, often write from the man's point of view, as a man can
write from a woman's, and it is not only in "Assurance" that
Emma Lazarus has done this. "Prothalamion," three unre-
printed sonnets, traces a young woman's emotions from
"First Love" to "Marriage Bells," and if the glorification of
motherhood which appears frequently seems unusual in a
spinster-poet, the probable explanation is her deep sympathy with her own mother. Vogel is right also when he says
that the stanza he quotes from another uncollected poem,
"Teresa di Faenza," is virtually indistinguishable from the
work of Elizabeth Barrett Browning:

What could I bring in dower? A restless heart,
As eager, ardent, hungry, as his own,
Face burned pale alive by our Southern sun,

A mind long used to musings, grave, apart.
Gold, noble name of fame I ne'er regret,
Albeit all are lacking; but the glow
Of Spring-like beauty, but the overflow
Of simple, youthful joy. And yet — and yet —
A proud voice whispers: Vain may be his quest,
What fruit soe'er he pluck, what laurel green,
Through all the world, for just this prize unseen
I in my deep heart harbor quite unguessed:
I alone know what full hands I would bring
Were I to lay my wealth before my king.[7]

IV

But what of the world outside aesthetic and personal considerations? What did it mean to Emma Lazarus as a writer and
as a woman?

Though she was not yet twelve when it began, the Civil
War inspired some of her first poetic efforts, and her record
in this connection is interesting and curious. "Brevet Briga-
dier-General Frank Winthrop" is a conventional lament for
a dead warrior. There is no reason to suppose that the writer
knew him or that he meant anything to her personally; she
probably used him as a type or symbol of the life that was
being taken by the war, but her two poems about John
Wilkes Booth—"April 27th, 1865" and "The Mother's
Prayer"—are among the most unusual of all those inspired
by the conflict. The bulk of the first, which is much the longer and more ambitious of the two, is given up to Booth's
own words or thoughts as he flees from his pursuers. Emma
does not attempt to justify him; each division of his lamenta-
tion is followed by the refrain:

> Go forth! Thou shalt have here no rest again,
> For thy brow is marked with the brand of Cain.

But she does enter into his feelings and think his thoughts
after him, and the reader is made to feel the pity which must
be awakened in all decent human beings by the thought of
any creature in extremis, no matter what his sins.

> "Oh, where can I lay my aching head?"
> The weary-worn fugitive sadly said.

The conclusion, recording Booth's death by rifle shot, is straight narrative, after which

> A prayer ascends to high Heaven's gate
> For his soul, —O God, be it not too late!

In the wholly sympathetic "Mother's Prayer," the poet attempts to express the emotions of the assassin's mother.

Outside the Booth poems, the most interesting of the Civil War pieces is "Heroes, which gives due meed of praise to those who died in battle but reserves most of its space and sympathy for those who survived into a life of toil on western plains or in city factories or, worse still, had to live "maimed, helpless, lingering still through suffering years." Eve Merriam rightly describes this as a truly mature point of view, and though "The Banner of the Jew" and "Bar Kochba" do not seem exactly pacifist poems, "The Crowing of the Cock" ends by declaring of the wronged Jew that

> The angry sword he will not whet,
> His nobler task is — to forget.

Though Emma Lazarus always insisted that she could not write upon an assigned subject (this was even her initial reaction to the suggestion that she produce the Statue of Liberty poem), she did not entirely avoid occasional poetry. Her occasional poems were not all devoted to military or political events, but she did lament the assassination of President Garfield and of Czar Alexander II, which left her feeling

> Bowed earthward, red with shame, to see such wrong
> Prorogue Love's cause and Truth's — God knows how long!

The most interesting thing about "Destiny," which comprises two sonnets inspired by the death of Napoleon III's son in a British regiment in Africa, is the way its conclusion shows the writer's bookish orientation:

> Enmeshed in toils ambitious, not thine own,
> Immortal, loved boy-Prince, thou tak'st thy stand
> With early doomed Don Carlos, hand in hand
> With mild-browed Arthur, Geoffrey's murdered son.
> Louis the Dauphin lifts his thorn-ringed head,
> And welcomes thee, his brother, 'mongst the dead.

She had some acquaintance with Henry George, who sent her a copy of *Progress and Poverty*, about which she wrote a sonnet imaging the age they were both living in as "richer than Cleopatra's barge of gold." It is "manned by demigods," and it carries

> freight
> Of priceless marvels. But where yawns the hold
> In that deep reeking hell, what slaves be they,
> Who feed the cavernous monster, pant and sweat,
> Or know if overhead reign night or day?

This is not exactly "refined" poetic diction for what the writer's contemporaries maddeningly described as a "poetess," but perhaps she had learned from Chaucer that one needs vulgar words to describe vulgar—and wicked—things.

Since she seems to have found George's argument unanswerable, perhaps we should not be surprised to find her responding warmly to William Morris's socialism also. In her article on Morris she acknowledges that his views might appear "wild and visionary" to outsiders and that in America, where "the need for higher culture, finer taste, more solidly constructed bases is so much more conspicuous than the inequality of conditions," it was natural to shrink from "the communistic enthusiast," but the situation was different in England, where "the pressure of that densely crowded population upon the means of subsistence is so strenuous and painful that the humane onlooker . . . is liable to be carried away by excess of sympathy." And if this seems a cautious approach, she goes considerably further in "The Jewish Problem," where she sees labor and capital "arming for a supreme conflict." At present "religious intolerance and race-antipathy are giving place to an equally bitter and dangerous social enmity." Generally speaking, she thought Jews broadly representative of liberalism and revolution in Germany and Russia and of conservatism and capital in England and America. The idea that modern "socialism and humanitarianism" derive from the New Testament as against the Old she rejected decidedly. Christianity was otherworldly; it held out the Kingdom of Heaven as "a glittering dream of suffering humanity" and enjoined "the vocation of the mystic, the spiritualist, the idealist" upon all, making little or no provision for the here and now.

On the other hand, the very latest reforms urged by political economists, in view of the misery of the lower classes, are established by the Mosaic Code, which formulated the principle of the rights of labor, denying the right of private property in land, asserting that the corners of the field, the gleanings of the harvest belonged in *justice*, not in *charity*, to the poor and the stranger; and that man owed a duty, not only to all humanity, but even to the beast of the field, and "the ox that treads the corn." In accordance with these principles we find the fathers of modern socialism to be three Jews–Ferdinand Lassalle, Karl Marx, and Johann Jacoby.[8]

V

As a writer Emma Lazarus admitted influences from many sources. In "City Visions" she wrote,

> I will give rein to Fancy, taking flight
> From dismal now and here, and dwell alone
> With new-enfranchised senses.

She did this in many poems. "August Moon," "Magnetism," and "A June Night" offer excellent examples.

> Elves on such a night as this
>   Spin their rings upon the grass;
>   On the beach the water-fay
> Greets her lover with a kiss;
>   Through the air swift spirits pass,
>   Laugh, caress, and float away.

But literature meant more to her than playfulness. In "The Cranes of Ibycus" she speaks of one walking through the huge town but traveling at the same time "in an April land / With Faust and Helen." This, surely, was her own experience, for her whole life was interpenetrated with the kind of stimuli that being steeped in literature from childhood supplies.

In the beginning the classics addressed her more directly than her own religious heritage. In "Agamemnon's Tomb" she sees the ancients as

a generous-fashioned, god-like race,
Who dwarf our petty semblance, and who won
The secret soul of Beauty for their own,
While all our art but crudely apes their grace.

"Daphne," "Clytie," "Aphrodite," and "Penelope's Choice" appeared in her first collection; in the *Admetus* volume she treated the Alcestis and Orpheus stories more seriously and at much greater length and also derived "Lohengrin" and "Tannhäuser" from mediaeval sources.

English literature also brought important influences to bear. I have found no specific reference to Chaucer for his own sake, but her statement that William Morris had "that virginal quality of springtide freshness and directness which we generally miss in modern literature, and which belonged to Chaucer and Homer" shows that she was aware of his quality. *The Dance to Death* has a Continental source of no literary distinction, but Süsskind's defense before Tettenborn surely includes echoes from *The Merchant of Venice*:

Is not our flesh as capable of pain,
Our blood as quick envenomed as your own?

and

we must breathe as ye,
The universal air, —we droop, faint, sicken,
From the same causes to the selfsame end.

"Recollections of Shakespeare" in Emma's first volume is a kind of vision-fantasy inspired by Shakespeare's heroines. "The Garden of Adonis" in the *Admetus* volume takes its epigraph from *The Faerie Queene*, and Milton's influence is obvious in both "Admetus" and "Orpheus." Among later English poets, the influence of Browning's dramatic monologues appears strikingly in "Saint Romualdo" and elsewhere, but the Romantics were probably even more important. "Lucia to Edgardo" in her first volume derives from *The Bride of Lammermoor* or Donizetti's opera or both, and when she first saw Chester, the streets reminded her of "the scene of a Walter Scott novel." In May 1875 she produced a poem "On the Proposal to Erect a Monument in

England to Lord Byron." Rejecting "the foul weeds of hate /
That shamed his grave," she declares that England's, not
his, will be the shame if she suffers him to be forgotten.

Emerson was obviously the American writer who meant
most to her, but through him she came to know both Thoreau and Whitman, who must have influenced the uncharac-
teristic "By the Waters of Babylon." "In a Swedish Graveyard" has an epigraph from Longfellow's discussion of rural
life in Sweden. She was a gifted linguist, translating from
Petrarch, Leopardi, Victor Hugo, Alfred de Musset, Heine,
and others. Among the Continentals, Heine was obviously
the writer with whom she felt the strongest affinity,[9] but in
1876 she wrote Rabbi Gottheil that German prose was hard
going for her. Her translations have generally been rated
high by good judges. Under the influence of her increasing
interest in Judaism, she began to study Hebrew, and the next
year she was very proud of having translated a poem from
the Hebrew. Up to this time all her translations from Hebrew poets had been made from German texts.

Emma Lazarus seems never to have made a systematic attempt to formulate a literary theory, but she knew what she
believed both about individual writers and general principles. In her correspondence with John Burroughs, she criticized both Matthew Arnold (whom she considered cold,
intellectually narrow, and lacking in spontaneity) and Carlyle; Burroughs defended Carlyle, admitting the justice of
some of her strictures but regretting that she could not see
anything more than that in him. In some moods she could
assume a stance that would infuriate the feminists of today,
as in "Echoes":

> Late-born and woman-souled I dare not hope
> The freshness of the elder lays, the might
> Of manly modern passion shall alight
> Upon my Muse's lips . . .

But she was not always so apologetic. Like Wordsworth, she
was sure that poetry came from emotion recollected in tran-
quility, but there was never any doubt in her mind that the
emotion must have been genuinely there. As she puts it in
"Life and Art":

> Not while the fever of the blood is strong,
> The heart throbs loud, the eyes are veiled, no less
> With passion than with tears, the Muse shall bless
> The poet-soul to help and soothe with song.
> Not then she bids his trembling lips express
> The aching gladness, the voluptuous pain.
> Life is his poem then; flesh, sense, and brain
> One full-stringed lyre attuned to happiness.
> But when the dream is done, the pulses full,
> The day's illusion with the day's sun set,
> He, lonely in the twilight, sees the pale
> Divine Consoler, featured like Regret,
> Enter and clasp his hand and kiss his brow.
> Then, his lips ope to sing—as mine do now.

Moreover, despite all her reserves in private life, she understood the need for communication between human beings and knew too that poetry can perform a very important function in meeting it, sometimes all the more effectively with those who cannot achieve this in any other way. As she puts it in "Sympathy":

> Therefore I dare reveal my private woe,
> The secret blots of my imperfect heart,
> Nor strive to shrink or swell mine own desert,
> Nor beautify nor hide. For this I know,
> That even as I am, thou also art.
> Thou past heroic forms unmoved shalt go,
> To pause and hide with me, to whisper low:
> "Not I alone am weak, not I apart
> Must suffer, struggle, conquer day by day.
> Here is my very cross by strangers borne,
> Here is my bosom-sin wherefrom I pray
> Hourly deliverance—this my rose, my thorn.
> This woman my soul's need can understand,
> Stretching o'er silent gulfs her sister hand."

Being more interested in literature than in theories about literature, Emma Lazarus was not overfond of critical classifications, but as she grew older and responded more passionately to the life around her, she would seem to have veered away somewhat from her early devotion to the classics.[10] Moderns who oppose romanticism to realism (a term which the nineteenth century added to the critical vocabulary) may be startled when, in her study of Ludwig Barnay, she speaks of the "romantic, realistic method, as opposed to the classic and antique," seeing "the great romantic revival in literature initiated by Rousseau and his followers" and developed by Goethe, Byron, Scott, and others as "but the protest of truth, nature, and realism, against cant in morals and the artificial in art." But it is at least interesting that the most determined modern critical enemy of what he called "Rousseau and Romanticism," Harvard's Irving Babbitt, should also have seen romanticism and realism as the related faces of the same coin, even when the latter ran over into its more extreme form, naturalism. In "August Moon" Emma calls for a poet who shall not only celebrate the real but reconcile religion and science:

> He shall be of bards the king,
> Who, in worthy verse, shall sing
> All the conquests of the hour,
> Stealing no fictitious power
> From the classic types outworn,
> But his rhythmic line adorn
> With the marvels of the real.
> He the baseless feud shall heal
> That estrangeth wide apart
> Science from her sister Art.

She warmly admired William Morris because he had managed to combine in his life the poet's passion for beauty with earnest labor in behalf of social amelioration, and as she contemplated his work, she understood, more clearly than ever before, that unless it is "balanced by a sound and earnest intelligence" and "a burning desire to bring all classes of humanity under its benign influence," the devotion to beauty alone "is apt to degenerate into a sickly and selfish aestheticism."

This side of her temperament led Emma Lazarus in the direction of literary nationalism. In "How Long?" she calls almost shrilly for American emancipation from foreign, especially British, models.

> How long, and yet how long,
> Our leaders will we hail from over seas,

> Masters and kings from feudal monarchies,
>   And mock their ancient song .
> With echoes weak of foreign melodies?

>   That distant isle, mist-wreathed,
> Mantled in unimaginable green,
> Too long hath been our mistress and our queen.
>   Our fathers have bequeathed
> Too deep a love for her, our heart within.

We "may not sigh / For lands beyond the inexorable main."
If "our noble scenes have yet no history," then our lives
must give them "all nobler charms than those that meet the
eye," and if this is an "aim austere," it still "opens new vis-
tas, and a pathway clear." In 1881 she told Higginson that
she saw signs of "fresh vitality" everywhere in American literature and that she did not share "the 'low down' estimate"
of it entertained by "the Anglo-American and half-informed
Englishman," and this point of view was developed and defended nobly in an unsigned article on "American Literature" in the *Critic*, published that same year,[11] in which she
took on George Edward Woodberry without gloves and
severely criticized the strictures on American literature he
had entered in a *Fortnightly* article. She was willing to grant
that Longfellow, whom she admired in many aspects, had
looked backwards toward our European heritage, but in the
work of her beloved Emerson she saw "the flowering of a
distinctively American school of thought and habit of life,"
and to her way of thinking the same tendencies appeared
in Thoreau, Hawthorne, Whitman, Lowell, Holmes, Bret
Harte, and others.[12]

VI

Emma Lazarus's relief, rehabilitation, and propaganda
work in behalf of distressed Jews during her later years was
of course a powerful influence in turning her away from
books to life as a source of inspiration. Though there has
been some controversy as to how early her decided consciousness of her Jewish heritage developed,[13] there can be
no question that it was tremendously stimulated by the per-

secutions which began in 1881. Though her uncle J. J. Lyons was a rabbi, she did not grow up in a religious family; the allegiance of the thoroughly cosmopolitan Lazaruses to the synagogue to which they formally adhered was pretty perfunctory. Her sister Josephine says specifically that Emma received no "positive or effective religious training" at home and that "it was only during her childhood and earliest years that she attended the synagogue," afterwards abandoning "the prescribed rites and usages" as a relic of the past which had, so far as she could see, "no bearing on modern life" and that "the first great moral revelation of her life" came with her discovery of Emerson. In 1877 she told Rabbi Gottheil that though she was loyal to her race, her religious convictions, "if such they can be called," had set her somewhat apart from her people, and she said practically the same thing to the Gentile E. C. Stedman when he urged distinctively Jewish subjects upon her as a writer. She was "proud of her blood and lineage," but "the Hebrew ideals did not appeal to her," to which Stedman replied that he "envied her the inspiration she might derive from them." In her late essay on Longfellow, she objects to his poem, "The Jewish Cemetery at Newport," because, though tenderly sympathetic, it sees no future for the Jewish people as a people, but her own earliest poem on a Jewish subject, "In the Jewish Synagogue at Newport," expressed precisely the same point of view.

> No signs of life are here; the very prayers
> Inscribed around are in a language dead;
> The light of the "perpetual lamp" is spent
> That an undying radiance was to shed.

All the Jewish rites can do now is to recall Bible times, and their sacredness consists in that:

> Now as we gaze, in this new world of light,
> Upon this relic of the days of old,
> The present vanishes, and tropic bloom
> And Eastern towns and temples we behold.

When Emma visited in Concord, however, Ellen Emerson found her "a real unconverted Jew (who had no objection to

45

calling herself one, and talked freely about 'our church' and 'we Jews')." But if this indicated a stage on the road of Emma's Jewish pilgrimage, it still left her far from the heroine of *The Dance to Death* as she faces martyrdom:

> "I am all Israel's now—till this cloud pass,
> I have no thought, no passion, no desire,
> Save for my people."

The Americanized, cosmopolitan, comfortably established Sephardic and Ashkenazic Jews of the nineteenth century did not always welcome what Emma Lazarus herself called those who crawled "blinking forth from the loathsome recesses of the Jewry" of Russia and Poland in the eighties, and it must have been harder for this sensitive, refined, sheltered, reserved, and highly aesthetic woman to do so than it would have been for many others. Nevertheless, she did it. She visited the immigrants' camp on Wake Island in the East River and interested herself in such mundane matters as food, housing, and sanitation. Convinced that "antipathy to manual labor" was "one of the great social diseases of our age and country" for Gentiles as well as Jews, she knew that the problem for the latter had been compounded because for so long and in so many countries they had been prevented from owning land and had found so many occupations closed to them. "Upon every Jewish school and asylum in the land, religious or secular," she wrote, "should be grafted a system of instruction in some branch of productive industry." So she became one of the founders of the Hebrew Technical Institute and allied herself with the efforts of the Hebrew Emigrant Aid Society to set up an agricultural colony in New Jersey. "The herdsman of Canaan and the seed of Jerusalem's royal shepherd," she wrote in "By the Waters of Babylon," "renew their youth amid the pastoral plains of Texas and the golden valleys of the Sierras." Finally, she became a Zionist before the word Zionism had been invented, the advocate of a Jewish homeland, not for American Jews, who already possessed "the double consciousness of the American and the Jew," but to take care of their less fortunate coreligionists in other lands, so that they should never again need to face such horrors as had flared in the eighties and given Emma herself a new purpose in life.

Was the basic motivating force racial, religious, or humanitarian? On first consideration one is tempted to reply that it was more racial than religious and as much humanitarian as either. (She herself called Heine "a Jew with the mind of a Greek" and said that his sympathy with Jews "was a matter of race, not of creed.") But the question cannot be answered in a word. Emma Lazarus responded warmly to the statement of former Secretary of State William Evarts at the Chickering Hall protest meeting: "It is not that it is the oppression of Jews by Russia; it is that it is the oppression of men and women by men and women; and we are men and women." At the same time she did remember that it was *her* people who were being oppressed and that if she owed them something as a human being, she owed them something more as a Jew. If a man lets his own children starve, one can hardly take seriously his concern for other people's children. "To combine the conservation of one's own individuality with a due respect for the rights of every other individuality, is the ideal condition of society, but it is a foolish perversion of this truth to deduce therefrom the obligation to renounce all individuality and this remark is no less applicable to nations than to persons."

Emma Lazarus knew that Jews are individuals. Their dualism was "the dualism of humanity"; they were "made up of the good and the bad." Yet she did generalize about them, and she did not always avoid the stereotypes that their enemies had developed. They are "naturally a race of high moral and intellectual endowments." But the Jew is also "a born rebel. He is endowed with a shrewd, logical mind, in order that he may examine and protest; with a stout and fervent heart in order that the instinct of liberty may grow into a consuming passion, whereby, if need be, all other impelling motives shall be swallowed up." On the other hand, "that the Jews are as a race shrewd, astute, and sharp at a bargain no one will deny." She even speaks of their "long-starved appetite for power." One well understands the indignation awakened by her article, "Was the Earl of Beaconsfield a Representative Jew?"[14] She begins amazingly by taking Spinoza and Shylock as representing the opposite poles of Jewish character, thus pitting an actual man against a character of fiction created by an Elizabethan dramatist who cannot possibly have known much about Jews except what he had read in the Bible and who may never even have seen one, and she concludes that though Spinoza's noblest characteristics did not appear in Disraeli, he still deserved to be called representative! It would take a hundred more years, she thought, to determine whether the Jews were capable of growth. "In the meantime, the narrowness, the arrogance, the aristocratic pride, the passion for revenge, the restless ambition, the vanity and the love of pomp of Benjamin Disraeli, no less than his suppleness of intellect, his moral courage, his dazzling talents, and his triumphant energy, proclaim him, to our thinking, a representative Jew." No wonder there were Jews who felt that with friends like Emma Lazarus about, they did not need enemies!

VII

There are both friendly and unfriendly references to Christianity in the writings of Emma Lazarus. I say nothing of her bitterness toward Christian persecution of Jews in "An Epistle from Joshua Ibn Vives of Allorqui" and *The Dance of Death* or her attack upon Madame Ragozin's defense of the pogroms in the *Century*,[15] for concerning these things all persons whose opinions could possibly be worthy of consideration must agree.

> This is the God of Love, whose altars reek
>   With human blood, who teaches men to hate;
> Torture past words, or sins we may not speak
>   Wrought by his priests behind the convent-grate.
> Are his priests false? or are his doctrines weak
>   That none obeys him? State at war with state,
> Church against church—yes, Pope at feud with Pope
> In these tossed seas what anchorage for hope?

In "Bertha" the abbot is a murderer, and Bertha and King Robert are excommunicated and their land placed under the interdict for having contracted an incestuous marriage on the ground that both had once stood sponsor to the same child in baptism, and in "Arabesque" there is a reference to Europe as sleeping "befouled with monkish dreams" during the Moorish period in Spain. I think there can be no question that Joshua Ibn Vives speaks for his creator when he denies a priori no miracle except the Incarnation, which seems to him a blasphemous notion:

> I say not therefore I deny the birth,
>   The Virgin's motherhood, the resurrection,
> Who know not how mine own soul came to earth,
>   Nor what shall follow death. Man's imperfection
> May bound not even in thought the height and girth
>   Of God's omnipotence; neath his direction
> We may approach his essence, but that He
> Should dwarf Himself to us—it cannot be!

It was Emma's opinion that " 'converted Jews' are probably not only the most expensive of all marketable commodities but also the most worthless after they are purchased," and as late as 1882 she objected to Rabbi Gottheil's reported statement that in America the Christian Church was "a noble and vital institution."

On the other hand, she uses Christian symbolism pretty freely. The uncollected poem "The Christmas Tree"[16] is purely fanciful, with no religious implications, and I suppose some Christians might be offended by the stanza in "Fog" in which both the child Jesus and the child Napoleon are used to glorify mother love.

> In his cradle slept and smiled
>   Thus the child
> Who as Prince of Peace was hailed.
> Thus anigh the mother breast
>   Lulled to rest,
> Child-Napoleon down the lilied river sailed.

But crown-of-thorn symbolism is used effectively in both "Epochs" and "By the Waters of Babylon": "Under its branches a divinely beautiful man, crowned with thorns, was nailed to a cross." I think no Christian poet has done a much better job of suggesting the healing, comforting effect of a cathedral than Emma Lazarus in "St. Michael's Chap-

el," and in the novel *Alide* both this and the winning atmosphere of the pastor's house are sympathetically presented.
Alide herself had "the constant chastity, the exalted faith,
the meek submission of the nun," though she found enough
scope for the expression of these qualities in the family circle
so that "there was no need for her to retire behind the grated
walls of a convent." As for the cathedral: "The sudden transition from the brightness of the noonday streets to this tender twilight, the vast space of the inclosure, the exquisite
beauty of the slender reed-like pillars supporting the lofty
vault above, the awe-inspiring associations connected with
the venerable Minster caused a deep religious adoration to
take entire possession of the simple girl's breast." It seems
entirely appropriate then that when Alide comes upon the
penitent Lucinda kneeling in the church, she should ask her,
"Are you not my sister in Christ?" but it is perhaps more
surprising that in her article on Disraeli, Emma Lazarus
should include not only Jesus but Saint Paul among the
great, "first-class," spiritually minded Jews.

The climactic position she gives Bayard's advice to the
artist Sergius Azoff whom he has just saved from suicide in
her short story "The Eleventh Hour"[17] would seem to indi-
cate that it expresses her own philosophy:

"I do not consider [life] either a boon to be eternally grateful for, or
a burden to be laid aside at pleasure. I consider it a difficult duty
which has been imposed upon us without consulting our desire.
The world seems to me an immense working-place, —a factory if
you will, —where each of us has his special task assigned, which he
cannot honorably shirk. A certain amount of labor has to be accomplished, for some universal end which we cannot conceive."

Bayard adds that he believes the truth about America to lie
midway between the roseate utopian dreams which Azoff
entertained when he came over and his bitter disillusionment later, and he is sure that art and beauty will ultimately
thrive here, though at present he cannot tell what form they
will take.

This seems more stoical than religious (indeed Emma Lazarus says much the same thing in "Epochs"), but I do not
wish to suggest that I consider her incapable of religious

feeling. In her first book, Niagara Falls is a great altar, where the earth "must needs send up her thanks to Him above / Who did create her," and "Remember" was inspired by Ecclesiastes 12:1. Judging by the number of times she refers to it, the Bible story that interested her most must have been that which relates Jacob's wrestling with the angel. "Influence" celebrates the power of a mother's prayer. The girl whose spiritual pilgrimage is recorded in "Epochs" tries "to reach with groping arms outstretched in prayer, / Something to cling to," so that she may lift herself "above disaster" and make her will "at one with God's, accepting his decree," while the mystic Saint Romualdo has achieved

> The power completely to detach the soul
> From her companion through this life, the flesh;
> So that in blessed privacy of peace,
> Communing with high angels, she can hold,
> Serenely rapt, her solitary course.

But the most interesting of all Emma Lazarus's poems from the point of view of her religious attitude and development is an uncollected piece called "Outside the Church," which appeared in the *Index*, an organ connected with the Free Religious Association of Theodore Parker and others, on December 14, 1872, and which Louis Ruchames has interpreted[18] as indicating that she herself had tried and failed to find the satisfaction of her spiritual needs in organized religion and found it instead in a Transcendental communion with nature.

> O Mother Church, what solace, what reply,
> Hast thou for me? No, I have stood within
> The cloistered limitations of thy walls,
> With honest efforts, earnest piety,
> Imploring refuge from distress and sin,
> The grace that on thine own elected falls.
>
> Wearied of these increasing doubts of mine,
> Harassed, perplexed, with one great longing filled,
> To hear the mastering word, to yield, adore,
> Conquered and happy, crying, "I am thine!
> Uplift, sustain, and lead me like a child,
> I will repose in thee forevermore."

All this to no avail. "To me the ancient oracles were dumb," and "the message did not come," though the speaker realized that others had received it. But upon his (or her) emerging,

> And lo! the spring-tide beauty of the earth
> Touched tenderly the chord unreached, unguessed,
> And all my spirit melted in a prayer.

Here, "in this free prospect, 'neath the open sky,"

> Here where I stand, religion seems a part
> Of all the moving, teeming, sunlit earth;
> All things are sacred, in each bush a God;
> No miracle accepts the pious heart,
> Where all is miracle; of holy worth
> Seems the plain ground our daily feet have trod.

In this atmosphere,

> All earth-born troubles wane and disappear,
> And I can feel, against my reveries,
> That not alone I stand outside the church.

Whether or not the persona in this poem is to be identified with Emma herself, it does not stand alone in the Lazarus canon. In "August Moon,"

> "Jove, Osiris, Brahma pass,
> Races wither like the grass. . . .
> Yet at Nature's heart remains
> One who waxes not nor wanes.
> And our crowning glory still
> Is to have conceived his will."

Tannhäuser, having been rejected by the pope, throws away the "leaden burden" of the cross about his neck on the Campagna and turns to what seems quite in harmony with Transcendentalism.

> "O God! I thank Thee, that my faith in Thee
> Subsists at last, through all discouragements.
> Between us must no type nor symbol stand,
> No mediator were he more divine
> Than the incarnate Christ. All forms, all priests,
> I put aside, and hold communion free

Beneath the empty sky of noon, with naught
Between my nothingness and thy high heavens—
Spirit with spirit."

Emma Lazarus had no patience with those of her coreligionists who clung to "antiquated ceremonials" and "repudiated with holy horror the word reform." These people might consider themselves the "props and pillars of Judaism," but to her they were its "living disgrace." For "if our people persist in entrenching themselves behind a Chinese wall of petrified religious forms, the great modern stream of scientific philosophy will sweep past them, carrying Humanity to new heights, and will leave them far in the rear." She offended the orthodox when she declared that industrial training was now more important for Jews than the Hebrew language and laws, synagogue worship, or circumcision. Her idea of the Sabbath was that it should be a day of joy, more like the Catholic than the Calvinistic Sunday. But if her views were Transcendentalist, they were also, to her own way of thinking, thoroughly Jewish, and she saw herself in the prophetic tradition. Indeed, Jews had less excuse for obscurantism than other religious bodies, for "the simplicity of their creed enables them more readily and naturally to throw off the shackles of superstition and to enlarge the boundaries of free speculation than any other sect. Considering their religion from the highest standpoint, their creed today is at one with the latest doctrines of science, proclaiming the unity of the Creative force." Was it not Isaiah who swept away "the whole rotten machinery of ritualism, feasts and fasts, sacrifices, oblations, and empty prayers. The prophets no longer call upon the children of Israel to go forth and make war upon nations whose lands they shall possess and inherit, but they are allied to the cause of 'bringing justice to the nations,' of 'establishing justice to the end of the earth' "?

The reader may remember that we asked ourselves awhile back whether Emma Lazarus's Jewish activities in her final phase were racial, religious, or humanitarian. In the light of such utterances as I have just quoted, this question both answers itself and loses its meaning. God chose the Jews, but

He chose them not for themselves but to bring the whole world to the knowledge of Himself; thus the idea of humanity "as a grand whole towards whose common weal every individual must strive . . . dawned upon the mind of man about two centuries before the birth of Jesus, and was the natural result of the fusion of Greek and Hebrew thought." Indeed, the God of the Hebrews has already become the God of "two-thirds of the inhabited globe," for what is Christianity except Judaism adapted to the mind of the West or Islam but Judaism adapted to the Arab world? And at this point racism in its ordinary acceptation melts away and religion and humanitarianism are one.

Amy Levy
1861–1889

I

LIKE MANY AMERICANS, I first encountered the name of
Amy Levy in the fine poem "Broken Music" Thomas Bailey
Aldrich wrote about her after her tragic death.

> A note
> All out of tune in this world's instrument.
>
> AMY LEVY

I know not in what fashion she was made,
    Nor what her voice was, when she used to speak,
Nor if the silken lashes threw a shade
        On wan or rosy cheek.

I picture her with sorrowful vague eyes
    Illumed with such strange gleams of inner light
As linger in the drift of London skies
        Ere twilight turns to night.

I know not; I conjecture. 'Twas a girl
    That with her own most gentle desperate hand
From out God's mystic setting plucked life's pearl—
        'Tis hard to understand.

So precious life is! Even to the old
    The hours are as a miser's coins, and she—
Within her hands lay youth's unminted gold
        And all felicity.

The winged impetuous spirit, the white flame
    That was her soul once, whither has it flown?
Above her brow gray lichens blot her name
        Upon the carven stone.

This is her Book of Verses—wren-like notes,
    Shy franknesses, blind gropings, haunting fears;

57

At times across the chords abruptly floats
A mist of passionate tears.

A fragile lyre too tensely keyed and strung,
A broken music, weirdly incomplete;
Here a proud mind, self-baffled and self-stung,
Lies coiled in dark defeat.

The "Book of Verses" referred to here was her second collection, *A Minor Poet and Other Verse*, which, to judge by the date written with his name on the inside of the front cover of his copy (which is now in the Houghton Library at Harvard), Aldrich had owned since its publication in 1884.

As to the "fashion" in which "she was made" we know a little more than Aldrich knew. The great Shakespeare scholar, Sir Edmund K. Chambers, probably after Aldrich her most illustrious admirer,[1] found in the face shown in her photograph "no special beauty, the brow and eyes burdened with a weight of thought, the lips set as if in some reticence of sorrow," but Harry Quilter thought he "had rarely seen a face which was at once so interesting, so intellectual, so beautiful, and alas! so unhappy." She was "a small dark girl of unmistakably Jewish type, with eyes that seemed too large for the delicate features, and far too sad for their youthfulness of line and contour."[2] The only photograph I have seen shows an oval-shaped face, rather large dark eyes, arched eyebrows, a fairly large nose, dark hair parted on the right side, and a straight but sensitive mouth. I should call her face sensitive and intelligent rather than either beautiful or plain.

There remains the act which Aldrich found "hard to understand" and which still puzzles us. The most authoritative comment here comes from Richard Garnett, who based his account of her in the *Dictionary of National Biography* on "private information."

No cause can or need be assigned . . . except constitutional melancholy, intensified by painful losses in her own family, increasing deafness, and probably the apprehension of insanity, combined with a total inability to derive pleasure from the extraneous circumstances which would have brightened the lives of most others. She was indeed frequently gay and animated, but her cheerfulness was but a passing mood that merely gilded her habitual melancholy, without diminishing it by a particle, while sadness grew upon her steadily, in spite of flattering success and the sympathy of affectionate friends.

To this the unsigned obituary in Oscar Wilde's magazine, the *Woman's World*, to which Amy Levy had been a contributor, added that "she was never robust; not often actually ill, but seldom well enough to feel life a joy instead of a burden."[3]

She was born, the second daughter of Lewis and Isabelle (Levin) Levy, in Clapham, on November 10, 1861, and died at 7 Ensleigh Gardens, London, on September 10, 1889, just two months short of her twenty-eighth birthday.[4] She studied for a time at Newnham College, Cambridge, where, if we may trust the testimony of her poem "Alma Mater," she was unhappy, but she afterwards remembered the city with affection.[5] She was well read in English literature and at home with both French and German and she translated the *Comme quoi Napoléon n'a jamais existé* of Jean Baptiste Pérès. She traveled in Europe and probably also knew some Italian. There is one Latin quotation in *The Romance of a Shop*. Whether the Medea piece which she called a "fragment" after Euripides (it is not exactly that but rather a brief play in the classical manner, complete in itself) implies a knowledge of Greek is not clear, but "Sokratics in the Strand" has an epigraph in Greek, and she quotes a line of Greek in "The Poetry of Christina Rossetti."[6]

At the time of her death she had published three novels: *The Romance of a Shop* (1888), *Reuben Sachs* (1888), and *Miss Meredith* (1889). Her first collection of poems, a thirty-page volume called *Xantippe and Other Verse*, was published at Cambridge in 1881. The title poem had already appeared in the *Universal Magazine* in May 1880 and was taken up into her first substantial collection, *A Minor Poet and Other Verse*, in 1884. She corrected the proofs of her final collection, *A London Plane-Tree and Other Verse* (1889), only a week before her death.

So little has been recorded concerning Amy Levy's life that, with her as with Shakespeare, we are dependent for our knowledge of her personality almost wholly upon what she reveals or what can be inferred from her own writings, a method of procedure which leaves us with more questions than answers. But questions can be illuminating, the effort is worth making, and her work is eminently worth examining. Her circumstances being what they were, she is certainly a minor late Victorian writer, but her accomplishment was impressive for one who died in her twenty-eighth year, and one cannot but believe that she might have developed into a really important writer if she had lived.

II

Since the three novels are less rich in self-revelation than the poems, we may well consider them first.[7] All are direct, simple, straightforward narratives, avoiding all unnecessary complications, and paying no heed to the sophisticated, self-conscious considerations of "method" which were coming more and more into vogue. *Miss Meredith* is a first-person narrative by the name character; both the other novels employ the omniscient author. For a Victorian, Amy Levy exercises considerable restraint in the matter of direct authorial comment, and what does occur infrequently is not particularly intrusive. Chapters, like the novels themselves, are short. The *Shop* has both chapter titles and epigraphs à la Walter Scott while *Reuben Sachs* has epigraphs only and *Miss Meredith* only titles.

The tone of the novels is much less melancholy, more bracing than that of the poems. Though the dark side of life is not ruled out, there is never any serious apprehension that the characters who speak for the author will be overwhelmed by it, and both the *Shop* and *Miss Meredith* have happy endings. The only unmistakable resemblance between the poems and the stories is that both are obviously the product of a sensitive and highly literate mind. And though both *Miss Meredith* and the *Shop* are distinctly "light," it should be stated with emphasis that there is never any suggestion of anything approaching the trifling or the vulgar which so generally disfigures this kind of fiction.[8] In the contrast it indicates between English and Italian marriage customs, *Miss Meredith* suggests the international novels which found their flowering in the work of James and Howells, neither of whom Amy Levy admired.

Gertrude Lorimer, the heroine of *The Romance of a Shop*, is "not a beautiful woman, . . . but a certain air of character and distinction clung to her through all her varying moods, and redeemed her from a possible charge of plainness." She writes, and among her unpublished manuscripts is a five-act tragedy about Charlotte Corday. Gertrude is twenty-three. Her sister Lucy, twenty, is "fair, slight, upright as a dart, with a glance at once alert and serene." Upon her Gertrude can always rely. Frances (Fanny), their half-sister, is "a stout, fair woman of thirty, presenting somewhat the appearance of a large and superannuated baby. She had a big face, with small, meaningless features, and faint, surprised-looking eyebrows. Her complexion had been charmingly pink and white, but the tints had hardened, and a coarse red colour clung to the white cheeks." Phyllis is "the youngest, tallest, and prettiest of the sisters; a slender, delicate-looking creature of seventeen, who had outgrown her strength, the spoiled child of the family by virtue of her youth, her weakness, and her personal charms." At the beginning of the book the already motherless sisters have just lost both their father and their fortune, and they set up a photographic studio. Phyllis dies of consumption, and the others all find husbands.

Their friends and acquaintances and the men they finally marry are all satisfactorily characterized. The most interesting among them is Aunt Caroline, who is perhaps a literary descendant of Lady Catherine de Bourgh. She is "a handsome person of her age, notwithstanding a slightly equine cast of countenance, and the absence of anything worthy of the adjectives graceful or *sympathique* from her individuality," for she "belonged to that mischievous class of the community whose will and energy are very far ahead of their intellect and perceptions."

I should say that *The Romance of a Shop* skirts melodrama and suggests that the author may have felt that she needed more incident than the normal lives of her protagonists could supply only when Phyllis elopes with a worthless, married artist and is brought back from his rooms by Gertrude. There is also at one point a report that Lucy's fiancé has been killed in Africa, but this turns out to be false.

Elsie Meredith leaves England at the beginning of her novel to teach English and music to the eighteen-year-old daughter of the Marchese Brogi at Pisa. The girl, wary at first, becomes very fond of Miss Meredith, and she herself is soon conscious of a "silent sympathy" with the old and withdrawn Marchese. But the Marchesa, "with her glib talk, her stately courtesy, was in truth the chilliest and the most reserved of mortals." The older son, Romeo, who obviously has his drawbacks as a husband, has a fat, friendly wife, Annunciata, who is often in tears. The younger son, Andrea, the rebel of the family, had cleared out in a huff, and the beginning of the book finds him in America. When his return is announced, the family promptly invites Costanza Marchetti, his hand-picked wife-to-be, to come to stay with them. "She was no longer in her first youth–about twenty-eight, I should say–but she was distinctly handsome, in a rather hard-featured fashion"; she is also distinctly bad tempered. Of course, Andrea–who looks enough like the Bronzino portrait of one of his ancestors in the family gallery so that when Miss Meredith first encounters him, she almost believes that the portrait, which has already fascinated her, has come to life–falls in love with her and she with him. The Marchesa tells Elsie that her son is "extremely susceptible" and no doubt honestly fancies himself in love with her. He will certainly "never take back his word, on that you may rely. But be sure of this, his life will be spoiled, and he will know it." Elsie's pride and her sense of honor force her to break the engagement, but when Andrea counters by announcing that if he cannot wed Miss Meredith, he will write off the appointment he has just accepted in England and return to America, his generally passive father intervenes. "My son, can you persuade this lady to remain with us? . . . You must forgive us if we are slow to understand the new spirit of radicalism which, it seems, is the spirit of the times. Once before our wishes clashed; but, my son, I cannot bear to send you away in anger a second time. As for this lady, she knows how deeply we all respect her. Persuade her to forgive us, if indeed you can." Perhaps the warmest admirer of *Miss Meredith* has been Harry Quilter, who found its art equivalent to Josef Israël's in painting and wrote of it with penetration and charm.

I have disturbed the chronology of the novels to take up *Reuben Sachs* last, for it is by all means the most significant of the three, and the only one that has been reprinted in our own time. It is also the only one which concerns itself with Jewish matters or affords any evidence that the author was herself a Jew. Her attitude toward Jews and Judaism I shall take up later in another connection, but the other aspects of the book fall for consideration here.

"Reuben Sachs," so the book begins, "was the pride of his family." He is a rising barrister with a fine scholastic record who might have aspired to the woolsack, but he prefers a political career and is elected to Parliament in the course of the novel. "Out-door sports he detested; the pleasures of dancing he had exhausted long ago; the practice of philanthropy provided a vent for his many-sided energies."

The novel begins as if it might be on the way to become something like a Jewish *Forsyte Saga*, picturing the Sachses, their relatives and friends, in a kind of cross section of the prosperous Jewish community in London. There are so many characters that here, as at the beginning of *The Forsyte Saga*, though the author has them all clearly in mind and differentiates their characteristics with ease, the reader must make an effort to keep them straight. But the author was right to use the subtitle "A Sketch," for she soon directs her attention and ours away from the clan to center it upon the ill-fated love affair between Reuben and Judith Quixano.

James Branch Cabell used to argue that a book which is named for a character has not been named at all; he broke his rule only with *Jurgen*, which he wished to call "The Pawnbroker's Shirt" but yielded to his publisher's objection. With Amy Levy's novel the label she used is clearly inept, for Judith is at least as important a character as Reuben, and though the action revolves around him, the reader comes to know her much better, getting inside her to a much greater extent, probing her passion for Reuben and suffering with her through its frustration. Indeed, during the second half, Reuben practically disappears from the scene. After she has lost him, Judith marries, not for love, a rather futile, silly Englishman, Herbert (Bertie) Lee-Harrison, who has been converted to Judaism.

The death of Reuben, reported to Judith by her imperceptive husband at the end, is one of the rare successful uses of surprise in fiction. Amy Levy had prepared for it by dropping various hints about Reuben's health and his overworking, but none of these has been heavily stressed. There has been just enough preparation so that we accept what she tells us but we still get the shock she intended, and it is necessary that we should have this in order fully to savor Judith's reaction. The whole incident is managed admirably.

III

What now, then, of the mind revealed in the poetry, with re-inforcement, wherever it appears, from other sources?

The obvious thing had better be said at the outset, though it must be documented more fully later. Amy Levy was, of course, as Chambers perceived, "a passionate idealist," a child, albeit a belated, disappointed, and disillusioned child, of the Romantic Age; this was her glory, and this was also importantly involved in what Aldrich called her "dark defeat." Only the disappointed idealist can suffer such disillusionment as consumed her; the "realist" has never expected very much; one must have asked a great deal of life to be as crushed as Amy Levy was by the best that life can give. She herself supplies us with an essential clue when she prefixes to one of the sections of her final collection what is at once the most idealistic and the most disillusioned quatrain in *The Rubáiyát of Omar Khayyám*:

> Ah Love! could you and I with Him conspire
> To grasp this sorry scheme of things entire,
>   Would we not shatter it to bits—and then
> Remould it nearer to the Heart's Desire!

Literature, art, and music—beauty in all its forms—spoke to her more clearly than anything else, but since the most obvious and omnipresent form of beauty is the beauty of nature, we must not omit this aspect, especially since, in her case, there is an important qualification to be entered.

She was a city girl, and she never forgot it; to the *Plane-Tree* volume she prefixed an epigraph from Austin Dobson:

> Mine is an urban Muse, and bound
> By some strange law to paven ground.

And in the title poem, "A London Plane-Tree," the author obviously feels a kinship with the tree she praises:

> Green is the plane-tree in the square,
>   The other trees are brown;
> They droop and pine for country air;
>   The plane-tree loves the town.
>
> Here from my garret-pane, I mark
>   The plane-tree bud and blow,
> Shed her recuperative bark,
>   And spread her shade below.
>
> Among her branches, in and out,
>   The city breezes play;
> The dun fog wraps her round about;
>   Above, the smoke curls grey.
>
> Others the country take for choice,
>   And hold the town in scorn;
> But she has listened to the voice
>   On city breezes borne.

Other poems in the same collection reinforce this one. One of Amy Levy's few really light-hearted poems, "Ballade of an Omnibus," is written from the point of view of "a wandering minstrel, poor and free," who is contented with his lot.

> The scene whereof I cannot tire,
> The human tale of love and hate,
> The city pageant, early and late
> Unfolds itself, rolls by, to be
> A pleasure deep and delicate.
> An omnibus suffices me.

Judged by the frequency with which she invokes them, the poet must have loved Gilbert and Sullivan, and I think we may be sure that her wandering minstrel was a legitimate son of Nanki-Poo. But we must not overlook "London in July":

> The London trees are dusty brown
>   Beneath the summer sky;
> My love, she dwells in London town.
>   Nor leaves it in July.
>
> And who cries out on crowd and mart?
>   Who prates of stream and sea?
> The summer in the city's heart—
>   That is enough for me.

Yet nature cannot be completely escaped even in the city.

> Between the showers I went my way.
>   The glistening street was bright with flowers;
> It seemed that March had turned to May
>   Between the showers.

Nor is it always gentle. The east wind can make the town look grey even when it has a blue sky over it.

> 'Tis the wind of ice, the wind of fire,
> Of cold despair and of hot desire,
> Which chills the flesh to aches and pains,
> And sends a fever through all the veins.

Nevertheless the last stanza of "A March Day in London" is cheerful:

> And o'er, at last, my spirit steals
> A weary peace; peace that conceals
> Within its inner depths the grain
> Of hopes that yet shall flower again.

Poems like "Out of Town" frankly acknowledge the beauty of the country:

> Out of town the sky was bright and blue,
>   Never fog-cloud, lowering, thick, was seen to frown;
> Nature dons a garb of gayer hue,
>   Out of town.
>
> Spotless lay the snow on field and down,
>   Pure and keen the air above it blew;
> All wore peace and beauty for a crown.

For all that, the call of the city will not be stilled:

> London sky, marred by smoke, veiled from view,
> London snow, trodden thin, dingy brown,
> Whence that strange unrest at thoughts of you
> Out of town?

And it is much the same in "The Village Garden," which, since it is dedicated to "E.M.S." probably refers to an actual garden and an actual friend.

> Fain would I bide, but ever in the distance
> A ceaseless voice is sounding clear and low; —
> The city calls me with her old persistence,
> The city calls me—I arise and go.
>
> Of gentler souls this fragrant peace is guerdon;
> For me, the roar and hurry of the town,
> Wherein more lightly seems to press the burden
> Of individual life that weighs me down.
>
> I leave your garden to the happier comers
> For whom its silent sweets are anodyne.
> Shall I return? Who knows, in other summers
> The peace my spirit longs for may be mine.

We must not, however, conclude that Amy Levy was unresponsive to the charms of nature. In the dedication to the *Plane-Tree* volume, the consolations which abide after all others have failed are the fair days of summer

> and more fair
> The growths of human goodness here and there.

"The Old Poet" resolves

> I will be glad because it is the Spring;
> I will forget the winter in my heart—
> Dead hopes and withered promise; and will wring
> A little joy from life ere life depart.

The poem ends:

> So once it was with us, my heart! To-day
> We will be glad because the leaves are green,
> Because the fields are fair and soft with May,
> Nor think on squandered springtimes that have been.

Similarly, "On the Wye in May" begins:

> Now is the perfect moment of the year.
>   Half naked branches, half a mist of green,
> Vivid and delicate the slopes appear;
>   The cool, soft air is neither fierce nor keen.

On this point too the reinforcing testimony of the novels is relevant. Gertrude Lorimer, the "inveterate cockney" of *The Romance of a Shop*, though fascinated by "the humours of the town" and "the familiar London pageant," longs for the country when she is under strain and finds her courage strengthened by the laburnum tree and other wonders of the April morning, and Elsie Meredith in Italy longs "with all my soul and body for the country" when spring comes on and loves the "great ilex tree" in the Brogi garden, "its massive green trunk old and gnarled, its blue green foliage casting a wide shadow. Two or three cypresses, with their broomlike stems, sprang from the overgrown turf, which, at this season of the year, was beginning to be yellow with daffodils, and a thick growth of laurel bushes ran along under the walls."[9]

In the last analysis, however, we must conclude that, however Amy Levy may have responded to nature, it did not suffice, as with Wordsworth, for example, to supply her with a religion that was mighty to save. In "In September" we read

> The sky is silver-grey; the long
>   Slow waves caress the shore,—
> On such a day as this I have been glad,
>   Who shall be glad no more.

In "The Birch-Tree at Loschwitz" she comes closer to pagan or Romantic nature worship than anywhere else.

> I lean against the birch-tree,
>   My arms around it twine;
> It pulses, and leaps, and quivers,
>   Like a human heart to mine.

But even this does not satisfy.

One moment I stand, then sudden
    Let loose mine arms that cling,
O God! the lonely hillside,
    The passionate wind of spring!

And I think final, conclusive testimony on this point may
well be drawn from the poem "A Dirge" in which she describes nature and its charms more fully than anywhere else
in her work.

> *"Mein Herz, mein Herz is traurig*
> *Doch lustig leuchtet der Mai."*

There's May amid the meadows,
There's May amid the trees;
Her May-time note the cuckoo
Sends forth upon the breeze.

Above the rippling river
May swallows skim and dart;
November and December
Keep watch within my heart.

The spring breathes in the breezes,
The woods with wood-notes ring,
And all the budding hedgerows
Are fragrant of the spring.

In secret, silent places
The live green things upstart;
Ice-bound, ice-crown'd dwells winter
Forever in my heart.

Upon the bridge I linger,
Near where the lime-trees grow;
Above, sweet birds are circling,
Beneath, the stream runs slow.

A stripling and a maiden
Come wand'ring up the way;
His eyes are glad with springtime,
Her face is fair with May.

Of warmth and sunward sweetness
All nature takes a part;
The ice of all the ages
Weighs down upon my heart.

IV

It is time to pass on from nature to art. The references to literature in Amy Levy's work, both poetry and prose, are so numerous that only a few samples can be given here. Her references to the Bible (both the Old Testament and the New) show an easy familiarity, and English literature is omnipresent. Shakespeare and Goethe are the writers of whom the "Minor Poet" in the monologue of that title takes his fondest leave, though he also mentions Theocritus and Heine,[10] adding "I've grown too coarse for Shelley lately." Miss Meredith, however, had not done this; for her the charm of Pisa was greatly increased by its association with the Romantic poets. The "Minor Poet" also pays special tribute to

> one wild singer of to-day, whose song
> Is all aflame with passionate bard's blood
> Lash'd into foam by pain and the world's wrong.
> At least, he has a voice to cry his pain;
> For him, no silent writhing in the dark,
> No muttering of mute lips, no straining out
> Of a weak throat a-choke with pent-up sound,
> A-throb with pent-up passion. . . .

The "wild singer" is not named, but Swinburne, of whom Amy did a good imitation in "Felo de Se," would seem a reasonable guess. Browning was, however, in her monologues, the most obvious strong influence upon her, though the only English poets whom she honored with complete essays were apparently James Thomson and Christina Rossetti.[11]

She thought that "a woman poet of the first rank is among those things which the world has yet to produce," for even Sappho's lyrics had "few strings" and "few notes," and Mrs. Browning achieved real excellence only in *Sonnets from the Portuguese* and "Great God Pan." She liked Christina Rossetti best when she was least "mystic, least involved— . . . simplest, most direct, most human," and her own tone being what it is, it seems odd that she should have found in her "that youthful exaggeration of sadness, that perverse assumption of the cypress." On the other hand, her reference in passing to Felicia Hemans as "a sweet singer,

undervalued in our day as she was overpraised in her own"
shows a refreshing independence of judgment and an intelligent realization that the latest opinion is not necessarily
definitive.

The essay on James Thomson is especially interesting because of the author's obvious temperamental sympathy
with her subject. Though she admits Thomson's "minor"
quality, she finds him "a poet of wonderful originality and
power" and responds eagerly to his "passionate, hungry cry
for life, for the things of this human flesh and blood life; for
love and praise, for more sunlight and the sun's warmth."
"The City of Dreadful Night" is a poem that "goes to the
very heart of things; it is for all time and all humanity." She
admits Thomson's lack of refinement and tells us honestly
that he is reported to have drunk himself to death, yet he remains for her "the image of a great mind and a great soul
thwarted in their development by circumstances; of a nature
struggling with itself and Fate; of an existence doomed
to bear a twofold burden." Whether or not she was wholly
right in these judgments, one cannot but respond to her generosity, nor, in view of her own fate, can one read unmoved
such a statement as "for, if one comes to think of it, it is appalling what infinite and exquisite anguish can be suffered
by a single human being who is perhaps sitting quietly in his
chair before us, or crosses our path on the sunny street and
fields."

I get the impression that Amy Levy cared more for Thackeray than for Dickens, though she was not impressed by
either as portrayer of Jewish character. When Elsie Meredith plans her trip to Italy, her sister Rosalind fears she will
be captured by an Italian Mr. Rochester, but Elsie reminds
her that she herself will have something to say about that
and adds that she has "always considered Mr. Rochester
the most unpleasant person that ever a woman made herself miserable over." In *Reuben Sachs*, Leo Leuniger expresses the opinion that Bertie Lee-Harrison must have been
shocked by finding the Sachses and the Leunigers "so little
like the people in *Daniel Deronda*," and we know that
his creator shared this opinion, for though she gave George
Eliot due credit for generosity and good intentions and

praised her as a novelist, she disliked "the labored jocose-
ness" and "the straining after pompous epigram" which
characterized her "later manner," and she did not think
the novelist knew very much about Jews. "We have, alas!
no M. Daudet among us. His mingled brilliance and solid-
ity; his wonderful blending of picturesqueness and fidelity,
have no counterpart among our own contemporary novel-
writers."[12]

The principal influence from the classics in Amy Levy's
work appears in her "Medea" in the *Minor Poet* volume.
This little drama opens after Jason has deserted Medea for
Kreon's daughter Glauké, who attracts him because of
his ambition to succeed her father on his throne. Medea
laments:

> For this indeed is woman's chiefest curse,
> That still her constant heart clings to its love
> Through all time and all chances; while the man
> Is caught with newness. . . .

By her children she sends poisoned garments to Kreon and
Glauké; then she kills the children. Jason decrees

> Let no man seek this woman; blood enough
> Has stained our city. Let the furies rend
> Her guilty soul; not we pollute our hands
> With her accursèd body.

At the end she goes forth "Into the deep, dense heart of night
—alone."

The most interesting references to art occur in the novels.
The Lorimer photographic studio is decorated with "a little
cheap Japanese china" and pictures from Dürer, Botticelli,
Watts, and Burne-Jones, all important in "aesthetic" Victorian circles. Judith Quixano's brothers are "two little dark-
eyed, foreign-looking children—children such as Murillo
loved to paint." The passion of the Slade school for Titian-
colored hair is mentioned at the beginning of *Miss Meredith*,
and I have already noted the Bronzino in the Brogi picture
gallery, a work

of considerable beauty, representing a young man, whose charming aspect was scarcely marred by his stiff and elaborate fifteenth

century costume. The dark eyes of this picture had a way of following one up and down the gallery in a rather disconcerting manner;
already [thinks Elsie] I have woven a series of little lessons about
him, and had decided that he left his frame at night, like the crea-
tures in "Ruddygore," to roam the house as a ghost where he had
once lived as a man.

The reference to *Ruddigore* may provide a convenient
transition to music. Leo Leuniger hums Schumann's "Ich
grolle nicht" under his breath, and though "Lohengrin" is
not essentially a poem about music, it takes its point of departure from Wagner's opera. Music causes sadness in "The
Piano-Organ," where a student, settling to work behind a
garret window, is disturbed by an organ grinder in the street
below.

> Grind me a dirge or a requiem,
>   Or a funeral march sad and slow,
> But not, O not, that waltz tune
>   I heard long ago.
>
> I stand upright by the window,
>   The moonlight streams in wan:—
> O God! with its changeless rise and fall
>   The tune twirls on and on.

But perhaps the most interesting reference to music is in "A
June-Tide Echo (After a Richter Concert)," where the poet
longs

> For once, for one fleeting hour, to hold
> The fair shape the music that rose and fell
> Revealed and concealed like a veiling fold;
> To catch for an instant the sweet June spell.

Dancing is of course closely connected with music, and
Elsie Meredith's first waltz with Andrea was "one of the intensely good things of life which cannot happen often even
in the happiest careers; one of the little bits of perfection
which start up now and then to astonish us." "The First
Extra" is called "A Waltz Song," and in "A Wall Flower"
perfect waltzing is praised and longed for, but this poem is
quickly turned into an exercise in déjà vu.

Somewhere, I think, some other where, not here,
In other ages, or another sphere,
I danced with you, and you with me, my dear.

I should say these pieces provide all the evidence we need to
be sure that Amy Levy enjoyed dancing, but the only reference of any kind I have found to games is in "A Game of
Lawn Tennis." That she had friends we know from Richard
Garnett's testimony, from what has been recorded of her
contacts with Olive Schreiner, Vernon Lee, and Clementina
Black, and the poems she dedicates by initials to what must
have been persons she knew and valued.

V

Did she have any extrapersonal interests, any views upon
public affairs? Clearly the bent of her mind was liberal and
humane. Her first published poem appeared when she was
thirteen in a short-lived suffrage magazine, the *Pelican*, and
in 1879 the *Victoria Magazine* carried another (reprinted in
the *Xantippe* collection) about a gypsy woman and her baby
who were "Run to Death" by hunting nobles in France.
"Wise in Her Generation" has references to blue-books,
poor law reports, and Toynbee Hall, and we know that in
1886 Amy was secretary of the Beaumont Trust, of which
Lewis Levy was president, and which was soliciting funds to
erect a "People's Palace for East London," which should
embrace a concert hall, library, technical schools, and other
features. As for her ethical standards, "Eldorado at Islington" is a touching little story about a poor family with one
child crippled. They believe for a day that the father has inherited a fortune from a long-estranged brother, but when
he returns from the lawyer's office they find he has rejected it
as "the fruit of cruelty and extortion; it was wrung from the
starving poor. It is money that no honest man can touch."
Surely her creator must have agreed with Gertrude Lorimer
of the *Shop*, who, when asked for her idea of good society,
defines it as "a society not of class, caste, or family–but of
picked individuals."[13]

If there is any one cause with which Amy Levy identified

herself, it is female emancipation. From Aunt Caroline's point of view the way the Lorimer sisters set themselves up in a business which necessitates their going out into the world and meeting men upon equal terms goes beyond verging upon the improper, and it is interesting that most of their customers think they ought to charge less than male photographers do. The heroine of "Wise in Her Generation" knows how hard it is for a woman to make her way alone "unless she happens to be Patti, or Lady Burdett-Coutts, or Queen Elizabeth," and in "Women and Club Life,"[14] Amy Levy herself sees the development of clubs as a response to the demand of women for emancipation from "the narrowest of grooves which have hitherto confined them." Though she can spare a sigh of regret for the old-fashioned woman at her best, she considers her too expensive a luxury for the times and even adds that she sees no reason to suppose that club women will develop the selfishness of their husbands and brothers!

Amy Levy's principal feminist document, however, is the Browningesque dramatic monologue, "Xantippe," one of her most ambitious poems, which attempts to rehabilitate the generally unadmired wife of Socrates. Xantippe had "high thoughts" and "golden dreams," a "soul which yearned for knowledge," and a tongue

> That should proclaim the stately mysteries
> Of this fair world, and of the holy gods,

but in the position in which she finds herself, she feels that her "woman-mind" had gone astray in thinking what are not "woman's thoughts."

Her marriage to Sokrates (as the poet spelled it) was an arranged marriage. He did not satisfy her dreams of "a future love, / Where perfect body matched the perfect soul," but she reached and strained "until at last / I caught the soul athwart the grosser flesh." She learned much after their marriage.

> But that great wisdom, deeper, which dispels
> Narrowed conclusions of a half-grown mind,
> And sees athwart the littleness of life

Nature's divineness and her harmony,
Was never poor Xantippe's.

Her husband (who is dead by the time we meet her) did
not plan it thus:

'Twas only that the high philosopher,
Pregnant with noble theories and great thoughts,
Deigned not to stoop to touch so slight a thing
As the fine fabric of a woman's brain—
So subtle as a passionate woman's soul.
I think, if he had stooped a little, and cared,
I might have risen nearer to his height,
And not lain shattered, neither fit for use
As goodly household vessel, nor for that
Far finer thing which I had hoped to be.

Once her wrath flared as he held forth to his disciples–Pla-
to with "narrow eyes and niggard mouth" and Alkibiades,

with laughing lips
And half-shut eyes, contemptuous shrugging up
Soft, snowy shoulders, till he brought the gold
Of flowing ringlets round about his breasts.

Sokrates expatiated upon woman's frailty, how

"Her body rarely stands the test of soul;
She grows intoxicate with knowledge, throws
The laws of custom, order, 'neath her feet,
Feasting at life's great banquet with wide throat."

But Xantippe's protest met only blank incredulity and
incomprehension.

Then faded the vain fury; hope died out;
A huge despair was stealing on my soul,
A sort of fierce acceptance of my fate,—
He wished a household vessel—well, 'twas good,
For he should have it.

Thereafter Xantippe devoted herself to spinning.

There is not a great deal of this kind of thing, however, for
essentially Amy Levy was a Romantic lyric poet and such
are necessarily largely committed to the expression of personal interests and emotions. There are several dramatic

monologues in the *Minor Poet* volume, but the later *Plane-Tree* collection is almost wholly lyrical. In "The Last Judgment," the speaker, a man grown old, approaches the judgment seat troubled because others bring

> Gold and jewels and precious wine;
> No hands bare like these hands of mine.
> The treasure I have nor weighs nor gleams;
> Lord, I can bring you only dreams.

Amy Levy's poetic imagination made it easy for her to think of herself as a man and old besides. "The Old House," whose use of the *Doppelgänger* motif suggests a familiarity with German poetry, ends with

> But who is this that hurries on before,
>   A flitting shade the brooding shades among?—
> She turned, —I saw her face, —O God, it wore
>   The face I used to wear when I was young!

Nevertheless, it must always be remembered that she was still young when she died and to this extent entitled to youth's emotions, aspirations, depressions, and dreams. If she was fond of calling her most ambitious enterprises fragments, her life was a fragment too.

VI

But what then was the cause of the despair that finally engulfed so intelligent and so high-minded a woman just when her career was going so well? As we saw at the outset, Aldrich puzzled over it; so do we; so apparently did the writer herself.

> O is it Love, or is it Fame,
>   This thing for which I sigh?
> Or has it then no earthly name
>   For men to call it by?
>
> I know not what can ease my pains,
>   Nor what it is I wish;
> The passion at my heart-strings strains
>   Like a tiger in a leash.

Basically, of course, it was the true Romantic, self-tormenting melancholy, asking more of life than life can give. Though this was perhaps more characteristic of French and German than of English romanticism, it casts its shadow over a whole generation and more, and its diagnosis is too complicated a matter to be undertaken here. It will be re-membered that Garnett says Amy Levy feared insanity; I do not know whether there was any basis for such fear, but Beth Zion Lask, who apparently knew more about her un-collected writings than anybody else, points out that, though she was a prolific magazinist, she does not seem to have published anything during 1887. In the poem called "In the Black Forest" she wonders whether her sadness has been caused by "the sloth and the sin and the failure" of the past, but this view is quickly rejected:

> They had made me sad so often;
> Not now they make me sad;
> My heart was full of sorrow
> For the joy it never had.

This seems essentially in harmony with the words of the sui-cidal hero of "A Minor Poet":

> I lament
> The death of youth's ideal in my heart;
> And, to be honest, never yet rejoiced
> In the world's progress—scarce, indeed, discerned;
> (For still it seems that God's a Sisyphus
> With the world for stone).

Nevertheless, it is clear that the speaker here has no faith in "progress," and it may well be that the poet had none either.

Suicide is the logical outcome of such depression, but hu-man beings are not always strictly logical, whether for good or for evil. In "Sokratics in the Strand," the ethics and the advisability of suicide are debated between Horace, a writer who finds a flaw in his machine and is inclined to try melting down the good material he believes it contains into the gen-eral crucible, and Vincent, a barrister who advises against flying in the face of nature, because she has "a little way of avenging herself." There is a first-person epilogue in which the circumstances of Horace's death are left obscure. "Poets and those afflicted with the so-called 'poetic temperament,' although constantly contemplating it, rarely commit suicide. They have too much imagination."

Probably Amy Levy herself knew well the ambivalence she described so well in "The Two Terrors":

> Two terrors fright my soul by night and day;
> The first is Life, and with her come the years;
> A weary, winding train of maidens they,
> With forward-fronting eyes, too sad for tears;
> Upon whose kindred faces, blank and grey,
> The shadow of a kindred woe appears.
> Death is the second terror; who shall say
> What from beneath the shrouding mantle nears?
>
> Which way she turn, my soul finds no relief,
> My smitten soul may not be comforted;
> Alternately she swings from grief to grief,
> And poised between them, sways from dread to dread.
> For there she dreads because she knows; and here
> Because she knows not, inly faints with fear.

In "The Promise of Sleep," however, death lures as a comforter:

> All day I could not work for woe,
>   I could not work nor rest;
> The trouble drove me to and fro,
>   Like a leaf on the storm's breast.
>
> Night came and saw my sorrow cease;
>   Sleep in the chamber stole;
> Peace crept about my limbs, and peace
>   Fell on my stormy soul.
>
> And now I think of only this—
>   How I again may woo
> The gentle sleep—who promises
>   That death is gentle too.

And surely the last poem in the *Plane-Tree* volume, "To E," is melancholy enough, coming as it does from a poet who killed herself a week after correcting her proofs. Here the speaker recalls her intercourse with two other people "three years gone by."

> Our Poet, with fine-frenzied eye,
> You, steeped in learned lore, and I
>   A poet too.

> Our Poet brought us books and flowers,
> He read us *Faust*; he talked for hours
> Philosophy (sad Schopenhauer's),
>   Beneath the trees.

But the poem ends ominously:

> On you the sun is shining free;
> Our Poet sleeps in Italy,
> Beneath an alien sod; on me
>   The cloud descends.

In the lovely "June," on the other hand, in which the poet laments an absent lover, she looks forward to a long life:

> O many Junes shall come and go,
>   Flow'r-footed o'er the mead;
> O many Junes for me, to whom
>   Is length of days decreed.

And in "Twilight," the speaker, though brooding over a recent death, reports that

> I leaned against the stile, and thought
>   Of her whose soul had fled,——
> I knew that years on years must pass
>   Or e'er I should be dead.

Finally, when Tom Leigh finds the "Minor Poet" dead, he muses quite in the manner of Vincent in "Sokratics in the Strand":

> Nay, I had deemed him more philosopher;
>   For did he think by this one paltry deed
> To cut the knot of circumstance, and snap
>   The chain which binds all being?

The testimony of the novels supports this point of view. Both Miss Meredith and the Lorimer sisters face their problems bravely (even the weak Phyllis boasts justly at the end that she does not funk). Gertrude Lorimer often walks at a swinging pace around Regent's Park "exorcising her demons—she was obliged, as she said, to ride her soul on the curb, and be very careful that it did not take the bit between its teeth." She never permits herself to forget that there is "only a plank" between herself and her sisters "and the pitiless, fathomless ocean on which they had set out with such unknowing fearlessness; into whose boiling depths hundreds sank daily and disappeared, never to rise again," and she feels sure that "to do and do and do . . . is all that remains to one in a world where thinking, for all save a few chosen beings, must surely mean madness." Yet she does not regret having been forced to face life as it is, for, "fastidious and sensitive as she was, she had yet a great fund of enjoyment of life within her; of that impersonal, objective enjoyment which is so often denied to her sex." *Reuben Sachs* is much sterner than the other novels, yet at the end we leave Judith, crushed by Reuben's death and married to a man she does not love, with "the germ of another life" within her, "which shall quicken, grow, and come forth at last. Shall bring with it no doubt, pain and sorrow, and tears; but shall bring also hope, and joy, and that quickening of purpose which is perhaps as much as any of us should expect or demand from life."

VII

It may be that Gertrude Lorimer was the kind of woman her creator would have liked to be rather than what she knew she was; it may be that she included herself among those to whom "impersonal, objective enjoyment of life had been denied"; it may even be that if, like Judith, she could have known "the germ of another life" quickening within herself, her fate might have been different. One must wonder then whether frustrated or disappointed love played any part in her tragedy. She herself wrote of Judith that "there is nothing more terrible than this ignorance of a woman of her own nature, her own possibilities, her own passions."

In the absence of biographical information about Amy Levy, it is impossible to answer such questions, and it may be that even to raise them, however sympathetically, comes under the head of unlovely prying. As a poet, surely, she was immensely concerned with love, but that is true of lyric

poets in general. As a poet too she concerns herself more
with aborted than fulfilled love (even Gertrude Lorimer, at
the beginning of the *Shop*, had lost a lover who was obviously not worth holding, "a fair-weather friend," who had deserted her in her family's time of trouble). But here again we
must remind outselves that poets in general have been more
preoccupied with the sorrows than the joys of love; the great
German Lieder and the imbecilities of Tin Pan Alley join
their testimony upon this score. And though it is difficult to
believe that Amy's love poems could have been written by a
writer who had never been in love, the fact that, like many
female poets, she could express the man's point of view
quite as well as the woman's must make us wary of attempt-
ing to trace a close correspondence between her work and
her life.

The stories too are relevant here. The heroine of "Wise in
Her Generation" wonders "sometimes, that we do not go
oftener to the bad, we girls of the well-to-do classes." When
such a girl is thrown into the swim of social life and contacts
with the men encountered there, she mistakes "the natural
promptings of her modesty . . . for resistance to this unknown force, which is drawing her to itself as inevitably
as the magnet draws the needle. With her little prudent de-
fences, she believes herself equipped for any fray; she feels
strong, and O God, she is so weak!" "Between Two Stools"
is the story of a young woman who did not know her own
mind. She rejects Stephen Brooke because she fancies herself
in love with Reginald Talbot, but when he has been won, she
discovers that Brooke is the man she really cares for and so
must reject Talbot too. "Mrs. Pierrepoint," more culpable,
sold herself to a rich, unloved old man who lived only six
months. A year after his death, she attempts to return to the
lover she had declined, Philip Quornham, now a curate in
Whitechapel, who rejects her.[15]

But the poems are, if possible, sadder. The lover in "To
Sylvia" says,

> I scarcely knew your hair was gold,
> Nor of the heavens' own blue your eyes.
> Sylvia and song, divinely mixt,
> Made Paradise.

But he also tells her,

> You've robbed my life of many things—
> Of love and hope, of fame and pow'r.
> So be it, sweet. You cannot steal
>   One golden hour.

In "At Dawn" love's fulfillment comes only in dreams:

> In the night I dreamed of you;
>   All the place was filled
> With your presence; in my heart
>   The strife was stilled.
>
> All night I have dreamed of you;
>   Now the morn is gray,—
> How shall I arise and face
>   The empty day?

In "New Love, New Life" the brown nightingale who symbolizes love is waking and singing within the poet's heart again, but the prognosis is not good:

> Love blest and love accurst
>   Was here in days long past;
> This time is not the first,
>   But this time is the last.

And in "Impotens" love makes the other dissatisfactions of life seem worse rather than better:

> The pitiless order of things,
>   Whose laws we may change not nor break,
> Alone I could face it—it wrings
>   My heart for your sake.

In "On the Threshold" the poet dreams that the beloved is dead.

>   I had crept
> Up to your chamber-door, which stood ajar,
> And in the doorway watched you from afar,
> Nor dared advance to kiss your lips and brow.
> I had no part nor lot in you, as now;
> Death had not broken between us the old bar;
> Nor torn from out my heart the old, cold sense
> Of your misprison and my impotence.

Except that in the novel the death is real, this might almost be the utterance of the heroine of *Reuben Sachs*. With this poem it is interesting to compare "In the Mile End Road," which of all Amy Levy's poems seems to me most like Hardy:

> How like her! But 'tis she herself,
>   Comes up the crowded street,
> How little did I think, the morn,
>   My only love to meet!
>
> Whose else that motion and that mien?
>   Whose else that airy tread?
> For one strange moment I forgot
>   My only love was dead.

"A Greek Girl," too, in her dramatic monologue, mourns for a man who has really died:

> Alas, alas, I never touched his hand;
> And now my love is dead that loved not me.

And again:

> For if indeed we meet among the shades,
> How shall he know me from the other maids?—
> Me, that had died to save his body pain!

Whatever else may be thought of Amy Levy's love poems, there can be no question that hers was a very chaste muse. The frankest expression of passion I have found anywhere is in the monologue "Christopher Found":

> This time of day I can't pretend
> With slight, sweet things to satiate
> The hunger-cravings. Nay, my friends,
> I cannot blush and turn and tremble,
> Wax loth as younger maidens do.

Yet

> Till the world be dead, you shall love but me,
> Till the stars have ceased, I shall love but you.

But much more characteristic—and even more touching— is the very Browningesque "In a Minor Key," which is written from the point of view of a lover who is not sure he still loves:

> And yet—and yet—ah, who understands?
> We men and women are complex things!
> A hundred times Fate's inexorable hands
> May play on sensitive soul-strings.

This poem closes as follows:

> I paced, in the damp, grey mist, last night
> In the streets (an hour) to see you pass:
> Yet I do not think I love you—quite;
> What's felt so finely 'twere coarse to class.

> And yet—and yet—I can scarce tell why
> (As I said, we are riddles and hard to read),
> If the world went ill with you, and I
> Could help with a hidden hand your need;

> But ere I could reach you where you lay,
> Must strength and substance and honour spend;
> Journey long journeys by night and day—
> Somehow, I think I should come, my friend!

VIII

If we do not know whether or not unhappy love played a part in Amy Levy's disillusionment and unhappiness, there can, I think, be no doubt that religion did. But before proceeding directly to this consideration, we must return for a moment to *Reuben Sachs*.

As has already been noted, this is Amy's only Jewish novel, but though such chapters as the one describing the Day of Atonement at the synagogue have clearly been written by an insider, it would hardly be an exaggeration to describe the general impression of Jewish character which emerges from this book as hostile. If Reuben and Judith are, with reservations, sympathetically portrayed, the Jewish community in general appears as clannish, self-righteous, and ingrown, shamelessly devoted to the main chance, and much given to gambling for high stakes. Sensitive to criticism from others, its denizens are divided from each other by "innumerable trivial class differences" and "acute family jealousy."[16]

Old Solomon Sachs, the head of his family, is "blest with that fitness of which survival is the inevitable reward. . . . If report be true [he] had been a hard man in his dealings with the world, never overstepping the line of legal honesty, but taking an advantage wherever he could do so with impunity." Reuben's mother "was an elderly woman, stout and short, with a wide, sallow, impassive face, lighted up by occasional gleams of shrewdness from a pair of half-shut eyes" and his sister Adelaide "a thin, dark young woman of eight or nine-and-twenty, with a restless, eager sallow face, and an abrupt manner. She was richly and very fashionably dressed in an unbecoming gown of green shot silk, and wore big diamond solitaires in her ears. She and her mother indeed were never seen without such jewels, which seemed to bear the same relation to their owners as his pigtail does to the Chinaman." As for the Leunigers, though they begrudge no money for food, clothes, furniture, or theater tickets, they regard every shilling spent on books as an extravagance. Except that he would not have considered it respectable to permit his niece Judith to marry a Gentile, old Israel Leuniger is "a thorough-going pagan"; "you need only marry a Jew and be buried at Willesden or Ball's Pond; the rest would take care of itself."[17]

As I say, Reuben and Judith are more sympathetically portrayed, but only up to a point. Judith is beautiful, and certainly the reader is expected to feel with her in her ordeal, but even here we must be told that her figure was "distinguished for stateliness rather than grace." She is also a "thorough-going Philistine" and "conservative in strain," and though she had enjoyed Shakespeare and Tennyson in school, she needs to settle down in Leo's room and read some of his books in order to realize that there was "something to be said for feelings which had not their basis in material relationships." Her religion she has accepted unthinkingly, and it has no strong hold on her. "These prayers, read so diligently, in a language of which her knowledge was exceedingly imperfect, these reiterated praises of an austere tribal deity, these expressions of a hope whose consummation was neither desired nor expected, what connection could they have with the personal needs, the human long-ings of this touchingly ignorant and limited creature?" She had been brought up to marry for interest, not love, and when she has lost Reuben or thinks she has and feels no choice available to her except that of Bertie Lee-Harrison, her mother is pleased to hear that she does not like him; in-deed she would be a little shocked if she did. "No girl likes her intended—at first."

As for Reuben, honorable though he is, "from his cradle he had imbibed the creed that it is noble and desirable to have everything better than your neighbor; from the first had been impressed on him the sacred duty of doing the very best for yourself," and though he cares for Judith, at least as much as he is capable of caring for anybody, he fails to pro-pose to her because he does not believe that a marriage with her would advance his career. When he is snubbed, he al-ways proceeds to wipe out the insult by making a conquest of the snubber. "Persons less completely equipped for the battle of life," writes the author tartly, "have been known to prefer certain defeat to the chances of such a victory."

One curious aspect of Amy Levy's portrayal of Reuben Sachs relates to his physical make-up. He was "of middle height and slender build. He wore good clothes, but they could not disguise the fact that his figure was bad, and his movements awkward; unmistakably the figure and move-ments of a Jew." And if we blink at this, we shall find as we read on that it is not accidental, for elsewhere his creator generalizes about "the ill-made sons and daughters of Shem." This was evidently a settled conviction of hers, for in what is perhaps her most significant short story, "Cohen of Trinity,"[18] she gives her villain-hero "a curious figure; an awkward, rapid gait, half slouch, half hobble." And in *Reu-ben Sachs* itself she tells us that "the charms of person which a Jew or Jewess may possess are not usually such as will bear the test of being regarded as a whole."

The best Jews in the novel are Leo Leuniger and Judith's father, who has been working for years on a monograph on the Jews in Spain which is obviously never going to be fin-ished. His daughter regards him rightly as "one of the pure spirits of the world," but she knows too that he does not count; he is quite ignored at the dinner of the clan that they attend together. "He was one of the world's failures; and the Jewish people, so eager to crown success in any form, so determined to laying claim to the successful among their number, have scant love for those unfortunates who have dropped behind in the race." Leo's devotion is to classical scholarship and his violin, and he is hopelessly in love with a Gentile girl, Lord Norwood's sister. Leo almost hates his people, who, "so far as he could see, lived without ideals, and were given up body and soul to the pursuit of material advantage." Even their religion, he tells Reuben, is "the religion of materialism. The corn and the wine and the oil; the multiplication of the seed; the conquest of the hostile tribes —these have always had more attraction for us than the harp and crown of a spiritualized existence." Reuben, who admits that the Jewish religion no longer remains a vital force in the lives of those Jews who have been enlightened by Western thought, attempts to make a stand for "our self-restraint, our self-respect, our industry, our power of endurance, our love of race, home and kindred, and our regard for their ties," but all Leo will yield to him is that "our instincts of self-preservation are remarkably strong; I grant you that."

"Cohen of Trinity" is the most important of the author's other writings about Jews, but it is not the only one; "Euphemia, A Sketch," which appeared in the *Victoria Magazine* as early as August 1880, has a half-Jewish, half-Gentile heroine. Cohen himself is a rather loathsome character, but though he feels out of place at Trinity, his difficulties seem more attributable to his personal deficiencies than to his race. He has "a glowing face" and an "evil reputation," with a "strange suggestion of latent force" about him, and the narrator says that "his unbounded arrogance, his enormous pretensions, alternating with and hampered by a bitter self-depreciation, overflowing at times into self-reviling, impressed me, even while amusing and disgusting me." He came to Cambridge on a scholarship but gave such a disappointing performance there (his own view was that the portion of his brain which had enabled him to win the scholarship had ceased to function) that he was dropped. Afterwards he astonished everybody by writing an able and successful book, but his success brought him so little satisfaction that he died a suicide. When he was reproached with crying for the moon, he defended himself by replying that after all the moon was the only thing worth having, and the narrator's final question about him is challenging: "Is it, then possible that, amid the warring elements of that discordant nature, the battling forces of that ill-starred, ill-compounded entity, there lurked clear-eyed and ever-watchful, a baffled idealist?" The *Gentleman's Magazine* gave "Cohen of Trinity" the place of honor in the issue in which it appeared, and the distinction was richly deserved.

Amy Levy's nonfiction writings about Jews seem to have appeared mainly in the *Jewish Chronicle*, and though in one of them she fears that she is not a very good Jew, they are marked by uncompromising honesty and an unyielding demand for intelligence, wisdom, and sincerity. In "The Jew in Fiction," which has already been cited, she asks for a truthful picture of "the Jew, as we know him today, with his curious mingling of dramatically opposed qualities; his surprising virtues, and no less surprising vices; leading his eager, intricate life; living, moving, and having his being both within and without the tribal limits. . . ." But "Jewish Children, By A Maiden Aunt,"[19] is even more significant, a wise, humane, and keen-sighted essay which, incidentally, shows that in some respects Jewish character, as manifested in family relations, has not changed very much in the last hundred years. Many marriages among Jews are still arranged, says the author, and "domestic affection" seems stronger among Jews than "romantic passion." "Love of offspring might, indeed, be described as our master-passion, stronger than our love of money, than our love of success." Jewish children, consequently, stand in considerable danger of being both killed with kindness and forced into a dangerous precocity. As a result, "the rate of mental and nervous diseases among Jews is deplorably high," and "there is scarcely a Jewish family which does not possess its black sheep."

IX

One can hardly believe, then, that Amy Levy found much spiritual nurture in Judaism, nor, though there is much religious coloring in her writings, in Christianity either. The sisters in *The Romance of a Shop* go to church on Sunday morning, and *Miss Meredith* opens "about a week after Christmas"; later the beauty of the cathedral at Pisa plays a large part in Elsie's surrender to the charm of Italy. Somewhat more surprising is one of Reuben Sachs's meditations over Judith: "If he had happened to be a doctor, Judith might have developed scientific tastes, or if a clergyman, have found nothing so interesting as theological diversion and the history of the Church." One story deals with psychic matters,[20] but it is impossible to say whether or not this indicates any belief in such things on the author's part.

There is a difference, of course, between a poem and a confession of either personal belief or unbelief; neither must the possibility of dramatic utterance ever be overlooked. It is "Magdalen," not the poet, who tells us:

> Death do I trust no more than life,
> For one thing is like one arrayed,
> And there is neither false nor true;
> But in a hideous masquerade
> All things dance on, the ages through,
> And good is evil, evil good;
> Nothing is known or understood
> Save only Pain. I have no faith
> In God or Devil, Life or Death.

Nevertheless, when similar notes are struck again and again in poems in which no obvious dramatic necessity appears, we are surely justified in suspecting that the ideas expressed were of some importance to the writer. In the *Minor Poet* volume, for example, we find "A Cross-Road Epitaph," with its grim German epigraph: *"Am Kreuzweg wird begraben / Wer selber brachte sich um,"*

> When first the world grew dark to me
> I call'd on God, yet came not he.
> Whereon, as wearier wax'd my lot,
> On Love I called, but Love came not.

When a worse evil did befall,
Death, on thee only did I call.

In "Impotens" the poet tells us that if she were "a woman of old" she would pray all sorts of prayers for her beloved but that now her "pitiful tribute" is "not a prayer, but a tear." And in the same *Plane-Tree* collection which contains this poem we encounter such utterances as

Our hopes go down that sailed before the breeze;
Our creeds upon the rock are rent in twain;
Something it is, if at the last remain
One floating spar cast up by hungry seas.

The secret of our being, who can tell?
To praise the gods and Fate is not my part;
Evil I see, and pain; within my heart
There is no voice that whispers: "All is well."

All's done with utterly,
All's done with. Death to me
Was ever Death indeed;
To me no kindly creed

Consolatory was given,
You were of earth, not Heaven. . . .
This dreary day, things seem
Vain shadows in a dream.

Your grave, I'm told, is growing green;
And both for you and me, you know,
There's no Above and no Below,
That you are dead must be inferred,
And yet my thought rejects the word.[21]

But I think the most cogent testimony to Amy Levy's unbelief—and to her agony—comes from "A Ballad of Religion and Marriage," which was privately printed by some unknown printer at an unknown date in an edition of twelve copies, of which one is in the Houghton Library:

Swept into limbo is the host
Of heavenly angels, row on row;
The Father, Son, and Holy Ghost
Pale and defeated, rise and go.

The great Jehovah is laid low,
 Vanished his burning bush and rod—
Say, are we doomed to deeper woe?
 Shall marriage go the way of God?

Monogamous, still at our post,
 Reluctantly we undergo
Domestic round of boiled and roast,
 Yet deem the whole proceeding slow.
Daily the secret murmurs grow;
 We are no more content to plod
Along the beaten paths—and so
 Marriage must go the way of God.

Soon, before all men, each shall toast
 The seven strings unto his bow,
Like beacon fires along the coast,
 The flames of love shall glance and glow,
Nor let nor hindrance man shall know,
 From natal bath to funeral sod;
Perennial shall his pleasures flow
 When marriage goes the way of God.

Grant, in a million years at most,
 Folk shall be neither pairs nor odd—
Alas! we shan't be there to boast
 "Marriage has gone the way of God!"

English poetry has achieved no more desolating summary
of the late nineteenth-century religious disillusionment. But
we shall read this terrible poem very superficially if we permit it to convince us that Amy Levy's was fundamentally an
irreligious spirit. It is not the pagans who feel that if God is
lost, all is lost. They live quite comfortably without Him.
Whatever they may think they "believe," they are the only
real atheists.

X

In his sympathetic but highly critical essay on Amy Levy,
Harry Quilter wrote that she had "perception and knowledge and intuitive feeling, sufficient to perceive [the world's]
incongruities, to estimate its difficulties, and to gauge its sorrows" but that "she does not seem to have arrived at that

further stage which renders such an experience possible despite its sadness—the stage in which the recognition of sorrow and pain turns freely, if not gladly, to action, which seeks to lighten the one and decrease the other." This suggests Gamaliel Bradford's remark about Henry Adams, when, weary of probing Adams's psyche for his own portrait of him, not long after he had made a similar study of the pioneer New England female educator Mary Lyon, he wrote, "Mary Lyon would have seemed to this wide seeker for education very humble and very benighted; but all Mary Lyon cared to teach her pupils was that 'they should live for God and do something.' If she could have communicated some such recipe to Henry Adams she might have solved his problem, though she would have robbed the world of many incomparable phrases."[22]

Coming as I did to Amy Levy fresh from my study of Lillian Wald, I find myself asking whether that indomitable spirit, who saw so much more of the world's evil than Amy did but was never defeated by it, could have helped her, but I pull myself up sharp with the realization that, no more than with Mary Lyon and Henry Adams, could she have done anything of the kind unless she had been able to make her over into something like herself. Whatever Amy Levy's responsibility or lack of responsibility for her final failure of nerve may have been, she surely paid a higher price for it than her severest critic could have desired. Neither Amy Levy nor Lillian Wald, nor Henry Adams nor Mary Lyon, put themselves together, and it is better to be grateful for what each has left us than to attempt to sit in judgment upon any of them.[23] As Goethe tells us,

> Eines schickt sich nicht für alle:
> Sehe jeder wir er's treibe,
> Sehe jeder wie er bleibe,
> Und wer steht, dass er nicht falle!

Lillian D. Wald

1867–1940

I

THE "D" IN her name didn't mean anything. It floated unattached in general space, signifying nothing except itself. Neither she nor her father had a middle name, and when, for some reason, they thought they ought to have a middle initial, both hit upon the same letter, "D." It was probably the only thing in her very meaningful life that had no significance.

This book opened with a study of the best-known early American Jewess Rebecca Gratz, who—long before there had been any scientific study of poverty and the social problems it involved, and when the relief of human need was for the most part left to private benevolence—did everything one woman could to heal the broken and comfort the bereaved. Her life overlapped by two years that of Lillian Wald, in whom, under immensely more complicated and sophisticated conditions, the same impulse widened into something which at last arrived at what it hardly seems extravagant to call social and political statesmanship.

But that is not the most significant thing about Lillian Wald. In her memorial article for Dr. Abraham Jacobi, she quoted his saying, "Doctor, please do not forget when you become so interested in your pneumonia case, that it is a little child."[1] She never did. Despite the immensely widened scope of her activities, she never lost the personal touch. Once she asked a young resident at Henry Street to look after a poor girl who was about to bear a bastard child. The resident objected that she did not qualify for this assignment, having had no experience in "case work." "Who said anything about a 'case'?" snapped Miss Wald. "I asked you to go to see a *girl!*" It must have been very nearly the only sharp thing she ever said.

Henry Street was not the first settlement house. Toynbee Hall was established in London in 1884, Stanton Coit's University Settlement in New York itself dated from 1886, and Jane Addams had set up Hull-House in Chicago in 1891. But when Lillian Wald went to live on the lower East Side in 1893, she had never heard of any of these. Nor, for that matter, had she any idea of founding a settlement house. People were sick with nobody to care for them, living in filth and squalor which not only doomed them but menaced the health of the whole city, and she set out to do what she could to relieve their sufferings and went on from there to make a start at relieving intolerable conditions. It was as simple as that.

Essentially it never changed, not even when she had an immense budget to manage. Only four years before she died, she told Jerome Beatty that if she were starting over again, she would do it the same way, "not taking time to worry and wonder about things but just going ahead and doing what had to be done." She never spoke of "the slums" or "the poor." She went to the East Side to learn as well as teach, to take as well as give. Her concern was not merely to "Americanize" the immigrants; she also wanted them to cherish their own racial heritage, which she saw as containing valuable elements for the enrichment of our corporate life. She did not condescend to even the poorest and the dirtiest. When people could pay for nursing or, later, for cooking lessons, she accepted payment to save their pride, even if it was only five cents. It was highly characteristic of her that when, late in life, she tried to sum up the effects of unemployment, she should have found its first and most tragic effect to be the loss of dignity it entailed, followed by the loss of home, disintegration of personality, and the conviction forced upon the rejected that society had no place for them. The number of delinquent boys and girls she saved for useful, sometimes distinguished, living is known only to God, but it must be very large, for she not only showed endless patience and sympathy in her initial contacts with such children, but

kept in touch with them through the years. She was the last
person in the world to boast (her only serious objection to
R. L. Duffus's biography of her was that it made her too important), but after twenty-one years at the settlement, she
stated categorically that no young woman identified with
the house had ever "gone wrong" in the usual sense of that
term. Often her trust was repaid in the unlikeliest places. She
was just beginning her work when, one evening, she could
not find the obscure flat she was seeking. Having nowhere
else to turn, she asked directions from a rowdy-looking pair
of young men on the sidewalk, one of them slightly drunk,
who first told her it was not safe for her to be out alone at
night in this neighborhood and then escorted her to where
she wanted to go.

Though she knew that there are parents who are not fit to
rear their children and should not be permitted to do so, her
first thought always was to keep the family together when
this was at all possible. Perhaps she derived her initial dislike
of institutional methods from her experience at the Juvenile
Asylum on 176th Street, where she worked as a nurse just
after her graduation. She even regarded Milton Hershey's
benevolence in establishing such an institution misdirected.
In her view, orphan asylums were outmoded; the thing to do
was always to try to get the child placed in a family, where
he could grow up under something approximating normal
conditions.

Helen Huntington Smith, then, could not have been more
right when she wrote of Lillian Wald that "she starts with
the concrete factor and works out to the general proposi-
tion. . . . She is a person to whom introspection is largely a
waste of time, and patter–including the patter of social
work–a nuisance." "We were driven to it," she herself said
of one step taken by the settlement. "We were driven to everything we did." One recalls Mary Austin's rejection of
what she called "the male ritual of rationalization," but
should any superior male suppose himself to have covered
Miss Wald's approach to either life in general or her specific
problems in particular by branding it "feminine," let him be
reminded that it was also thoroughly scientific, for what is
the scientific method if not the deduction of general laws

from specific data, collected and arranged? Lillian Wald applied this to more than settlement work. She put her whole career on the line when she opposed the entrance of the United States into World War I, yet the theoretical basis of pacifism never interested her. What she was interested in was any practical step that could keep her country out of *this* war, and it was thus that she escaped the futility of being enrolled with the great ineffectual army of those who oppose war *but*.

II

Lillian Wald was born in Cincinnati on March 10, 1867, the third of the four children of Max D. Wald and Minnie (Schwarz) Wald. Her forebears on both sides had been merchants, rabbis, and professional men in Poland and Germany, and both families had been in the United States since shortly after the revolutions of 1848. Max Wald was a prosperous dealer in optical goods, whose business connections dictated a removal from Cincinnati, first to Dayton and later to Rochester, which his daughter regarded as her home town.

Mrs. Wald was a beautiful and fantastically generous woman who might have been a New Testament literalist, for she gave to everyone who asked of her. When, toward the end of her life, she lived in the settlement house, she almost had to be restrained from giving it away piece by piece, and whenever a neighboring family was dispossessed she wanted to move them in with the settlement.

Lillian was sent to Miss Cruttenden's English-French Boarding School in Rochester. She studied Latin and spoke both French and German. When, in later years, she visited Russia and found it necessary to converse in German because she knew no Russian and her interlocutors no English, she was amazed to find a copious vocabulary welling up from within her. Having graduated from Miss Cruttenden's at the age of sixteen, she applied for admission to Vassar College but was rejected because she was too young, and she never reapplied there or elsewhere. In later years she manifested little sympathy with the American urge to send young people to college "regardless of scholarly ambition or aptitude." The idea of college as a trade school did not appeal to her, and she believed that "among aspirants to the higher degrees, one frequently encounters a narrowness of outlook and lack of information that amount to ignorance in an educated person's sense."

Until 1889 Lillian Wald led the normal life of a prosperous, cultivated, well-to-do young American of her time, devoting herself "to society, study, and housekeeping duties." In August of that year, searching for some more definite purpose in life, she went into training as a nurse at the New York Hospital. Because a patient thought she would be more comfortable if Miss Wald were present, she forced herself to watch an operation. After her graduation in 1891, she spent a year at the New York Juvenile Asylum and then enrolled in a course she never completed at the Woman's Medical College.

In 1893, while still in medical school, she was asked to organize home-nursing courses on the East Side, and there, one drizzling March day, she confronted her moment of truth and her destiny along with it when a little girl came to the schoolroom where she had been giving a lesson in bed-making and begged her to come to her mother, who had just given birth "in a squalid rear tenement, so wretched and pitiful that, in all the years since, I have not seen anything more appalling." She marked the importance of this incident by relating it at the very beginning of *The House on Henry Street*:

The child led me over broken roadways–there was no asphalt, although its use was well established in other parts of the city, — over dirty mattresses and heaps of refuse, . . . between tall, reeking houses whose laden fire-escapes, useless for their appointed purpose, bulged with household goods of every description. The rain added to the dismal appearance of the streets and to the discomfort of the crowds which thronged them, intensifying the odors which assailed me from every side. . . .

The child led me on through a tenement hallway, across a court where open and unscreened closets were promiscuously used by men and women, up into a rear tenement, by slimy steps whose accumulated dirt was augmented that day by the mud of the streets, and finally into the sickroom.

All the maladjustments of our social and economic relations seemed epitomized in this brief journey and what was found at the end of it. The family to which the child led me was neither criminal nor vicious. Although the husband was a cripple, one of those who stand on street corners exhibiting deformities to enlist compassion, and masking the begging of alms by a pretense at selling; although the family of seven shared their two rooms with boarders–who were literally boarders, since a piece of timber was placed over the floor for them to sleep on, —and although the sick woman lay on a wretched, unclean bed, soiled with a hemorrhage two days old, they were not degraded human beings, judged by any measure of moral values.

In fact, it was very plain that they were sensitive to their condition, and when, at the end of my ministrations, they kissed my hands (those who have undergone similar experiences will, I am sure, understand), it would have been some solace if by any conviction of the moral unworthiness of the family I could have defended myself as part of a society which permitted such conditions to exist. Indeed, my subsequent acquaintance with them revealed the fact that, miserable as their state was, they were not without ideals for the family life, and for society, of which they were so unloved and unlovely a part.

Out of this experience came an idea and a plan. Lillian Wald and another nurse, Mary Brewster (a descendant of the Puritan Elder Brewster), would move into the neighborhood, giving their services and contributing their sense of citizenship "to what seems an alien group in a so-called democratic community." "Red-cheeked and excited, almost too excited to talk," Lillian Wald explained it all one evening to Mrs. Solomon Loeb, who later told her daughter Nina (afterwards Mrs. Paul Warburg), "I have had a wonderful experience! I have talked with a young woman who is either crazy or a great genius." With financial backing from Mrs. Loeb and her son-in-law Jacob H. Schiff, the two young women settled in September on the top floor of a Jefferson Street tenement, and there they stayed until 1895, when the "Nurses Settlement" established its headquarters at 265 Henry Street.

Having suffered a breakdown in health, Mary Brewster

disappeared from the picture early and died while still a young woman. But soon there were eleven residents, and by 1913 the settlement had, among other things, seven houses on Henry Street and two branches, plus seven vacation homes in the country, with ninety-two nurses making 200,000 visits annually, and 3,000 people enrolled in clubs and classes. By 1916 the value of their property holdings was half a million dollars, and the annual budget for the visiting-nurse service alone was $150,000. Three years later, the thirty-seven residents were being assisted by 101 volunteers, and by 1932 the visiting nurses would be working out of twenty centers.

In 1902 a demonstration by Lina L. Rogers led the New York City Board of Health to establish the first public-school nursing program in the United States. In 1904 Lillian Wald and Florence Kelley founded the National Child Labor Committee. President Theodore Roosevelt was receptive to the idea of a federal Children's Bureau in 1905, but Congress dragged its feet, and the bureau was not established until 1912. In 1909, however, the Metropolitan Life Insurance Company was persuaded to inaugurate a nursing program for industrial policy holders, and this developed until soon 1,200 cities and towns had nurses working with insurance companies. A department of Nursing and Health was set up at Teachers College, Columbia University, in 1910, and two years later the Red Cross established its Town and Country Nursing Service.

The settlement was also drawn into activities and forced to take positions on issues that involved not only the Henry Street neighborhood but the entire city, the nation, and the world. As early as the Panic of 1893, Lillian Wald served on a committee engaged in trying to provide work for the unemployed, and there was much more of this kind of thing when the Great Depression began in 1929. During the epidemic of Spanish influenza which followed the war in 1918, the Henry Street nurses rendered heroic, almost superhuman, service. Five hundred cases were reported during the first four days of October alone, and soon the nurses were going out in shifts day and night, and volunteers were being recruited wherever they might be obtained. With Jane Addams, Florence Kelley, and others, Lillian Wald had organized the American Union Against Militarism as early as 1914, and when the fight to keep America out of the war had been lost, the Union turned its attention to the relief of war-related sufferings and the defense of civil liberties. After the war, it became the League of Free Nations Associations, a forerunner of the Foreign Policy Association, and, through one of its branches, helped to give birth to the American Civil Liberties Union.

In 1912 Miss Wald took her stand with TR's Progressive Party, but in 1916 she supported Wilson for reelection. In 1928 she supported Al Smith, a good friend of Henry Street, in spite of her disagreement with his opposition to prohibition, because she considered him a progressive on social legislation. She was friendly with both Franklin and Eleanor Roosevelt. A number of Henry Street alumni were prominent New Dealers, and Lillian was sufficiently captivated by the achievements of FDR's first term to support him for reelection in 1936. Since she died during the campaign of 1940, which again returned him to the White House, she was spared the full agony of his shift toward war.

Her health began to fail in the 1920s; thereafter anemia and a heart condition forced her to take frequent vacations and to spend much of her time at her "House-on-the-Pond," Westport, Connecticut, which she had acquired in 1909. She had been killing herself for years, working all day and half the night besides. Late in 1925 she had "facial neuralgia and shingles and tingling in my right hand and a kind of gone feeling," but the only thing she really worried about was that she did not know how much she could do; a few months later she wrote a visiting portrait painter that she had fallen down the stairs and nearly wrecked herself and that she was sure he did not wish to paint "a grand old ruin." On her sixtieth birthday in March 1927 she woke up with a cold and a cough and a carbuncle, but when, shortly thereafter, Ramsay MacDonald was taken dangerously ill in Philadelphia, none of her ailments kept her from going there to nurse him through his crisis, which of course further depleted her reserves. In 1931 she was forced to miss a meeting of the Women's International League for Peace and

Freedom in Washington, and in January 1933 a severe attack of flu further weakened her heart. By March it was a triumph to be able to report that she had been able to sit up in a chair for five minutes, yet in April she wrote, "Though I've had every ill that man or woman is heir to, my mind has not been less acute nor my anxiety less for the things we stand for." But she had reached a point where the weakened body simply could no longer obey the unimpaired mind and spirit. That same year she resigned as head resident at Henry Street, and in 1937 she became president emeritus of the board. Her death at Westport, on September 1, 1940, came after a long illness following a cerebral hemorrhage.

III

Though Lillian Wald afterwards thought of herself as having spent her early years as a spoiled child, it is easy to see now that they supplied an important element in preparing her for life. Her own protected, cherished childhood showed her what children need and how they should be brought up. Had she grown up in a less protected environment, she might never have realized how important play is to a child nor how imagination can be stimulated and horizons widened through contacts with art, and one whole side of the work of the settlement would have been handicapped in consequence.

Without her own childhood visits to the theater, for example, she could hardly have realized how much the performance of *Peter Pan* which Maude Adams gave for the East Side children could mean to them or how it might be cherished in memory as a vision of how good life can be. She herself had had not only the theater but books and music and much besides. As a child, she read Dickens and George Eliot, identifying herself and those around her with the characters in *The Mill on the Floss*. Her Grandfather Schwarz, who bought ponies for the children and built a bowling alley and a children's playhouse in the garden for them, loved folk tales and fairy tales, *The Arabian Nights*, *The Nibelungenlied*, and Schiller, and did his best to pass these tastes on. Lillian Wald never discarded the conviction that fairy tales were "an essential part of every child's education, and, for that matter, of every grown-up's sustenance." She granted that, in a mechanical age, it might be exciting to see a child working on airplane models or being able to identify the various makes of automobile from a distance, but if the price that must be paid for such interests came in terms of "literal-mindedness and stunted imagination," she thought it too high.

She began early to make an impression upon those around her. One of her schoolmates at Miss Cruttenden's in Rochester remembered the girl in after years as tall, beautiful, streamlined in figure, and extremely elegant when attired to go out to a party or a dance. At the time of the tenth anniversary of the Henry Street settlement, a newspaper reporter saw her as "a woman still in the freshness of youth: tall–a little above the average height–and well proportioned; an oval face crowned by dark wavy hair simply parted over a smooth, broad brow; eyes so large and brown and soft that they seem to look at you almost timidly. The mouth is tender, sensitive, sympathetic. The chin says, 'I will,' in every one of its firm lines." She was sixty-two when Helen Huntington Smith produced her *New Yorker* "Profile" in which Lillian Wald appears as "ample of build" and "responsive," and a woman who might have been called "motherly, except that the term implies a degree of softness, and Miss Wald, with all her boundless sympathies, is not soft." But perhaps the best tribute came from Einstein, as he left her after a visit only two years before she died. "I want to thank you," he said, "for your smile."

Beauty is in the eye of the beholder, but, whether or not Lillian Wald was beautiful, there can be no question that she had charm. She spent her life fighting intolerable conditions and opposing those who had created them, yet she seems never to have quarreled with anybody. She did not gloss over moral issues, and whatever her theology may have been, she never lost the sense of sin or the conviction that wrongdoing must be acknowledged and made right that has now become so unfashionable and for whose lack our society seems to be coming apart at the seams. "What has been written in the chapters of this book," she says toward the close of *Windows on Henry Street*, "will have lost significance if a consciousness of sin in our human relations and a quite genuine impulse to do better have not been recorded." But she also knew that people did not come to her primarily for her advice, and she doubted they ever followed it when she gave it. "What they really wanted was to tell their trouble—sometimes their crime—to someone who would forget."

Basically, however, she believed in human beings. When she first discovered the horrors of the East Side, she thought people only needed to be made aware of such things to do something about them, and for all her disappointments, she never really got over expecting this. With all the thousands of things she had to do, she could still always find time for little kindnesses—notes, remembrances, and small gifts. She was a good conversationalist also, and she had a genuine interest in everybody she met and a consequent ability to shift the focus of attention away from herself to the other person. Though she professed to dislike money raising, she must have been at it through all her Henry Street years, though she may have done much of it in a subtle or indirect way. It was said that it cost $5,000 to sit next to Miss Wald at dinner, and Felix Warburg once advised a man who had proposed going to see her to remonstrate about something she had done to write her a letter instead: "If you see her, you might change your mind. I have."

Jacob A. Riis said of Lillian Wald that "there never was a woman with her power of loving people."[2] On the morning of the day she died, she told her nurse that she was a very happy woman "because I have had so many people to love, and so many people have loved me."[3] But what she herself wrote of Jacob H. Schiff is perhaps even more significant in its application to the writer: "He loved his fellowmen and his keen mind was never obscured by his emotions. He gave both heart and intellect to what, I am sure, were the great interests of his life."[4]

In her own work this double emphasis was always present, and it would have been hard to say which aspect was the more important. Without the first she would not have cared; without the second, her caring could not have availed. Jerome Beatty described her as "a woman with a backbone of tempered steel, a heart as big as a house, and the courage of all the lions in Africa." There was nothing of the exhibitionist in her, and she never really succeeded in conquering her dislike of public speaking, but perhaps a trace of the old Adam (or Eve) does survive in her late saying: "I suppose one as ready to take up challenges as I am ought to think of retiring and live in a monastery somewhere safe from battles. Yet how I would miss not having a battle—and this from a pacifist is a confession!"

If Lillian Wald was ever in love in the narrower and usual sense of the term, no record of it seems to have been preserved. One writer, Blanche Wiesen Cook,[5] has advanced, rather tentatively and inconclusively, the thesis that she relied for emotional support and encouragement upon her women friends and associates. So I am sure she did, and this would have been a perfectly normal and natural thing to do, quite without reference to any of the specialized considerations which this writer just shies off from reading into it, but the weakness of her article is that it makes no allowance for what Lillian Wald may have got from such male friends and supporters as Van Wyck Brooks, Paul Kellogg, George W. Alger, Lee Simonson, Ernest Poole, Felix Warburg, Sidney Hillman, Graham Wallas, and many more. In her later years at least, Scotties possessed themselves of an important place in her affections, but I have found no other references to animals, aside from the ponies of her childhood.

Her biographer calls her "joyous, fun-loving, beauty-loving, . . . buoyant, charged with energy, alive with curiosity, eager to see and do," and one of her associates, Lavinia Dock, who knew her much more intimately, documents this view.

If there was even a tinge of melancholy or sadness it never showed. I never saw her dispirited or dejected or downcast. I never saw her show annoyance or irritation or anger toward any other person. . . . There was perhaps not a vestige of pessimism or gloom in her nature, no trace of discouragement, even. A seriousness, pity, compassion in the face of terrible deeds and world calamities, but always the steady, unaltered balance and poise of warm-hearted hopefulness and belief in human nature.

It was completely in character for her that even during the "jazz age" she should insist that "our much-criticized young people often gave better account of themselves than did their elders," for she knew that it was not they or their generation that had brought the world to the verge of destruction and that if it were to be saved, it would have to be they who saved it.

The one thing she could never learn was how to spare herself. She would run upstairs instead of waiting for the elevator and jump up from her desk, coming forward to greet her visitors with "gay voice, welcoming smile, cordial gesture" instead of waiting for them to approach her. She refused to allow a friend to buy her a motor car so that she might get about New York with less trouble. She could not, she thought, do with "so much luxury"; it would be time enough to think about that when she was so decrepit that she could not jump on and off the streetcars. Until her associates had it taken away from her when her health was breaking, she slept by the telephone on a screened-in porch above her little garden, where anybody who wanted her could call her at any hour.

Like her great friend and contemporary Jane Addams, she always insisted that she was not living a life of sacrifice, but she did sometimes worry that she might be asking too much of her associates. This thought came to her one night at the opera, and she found it "so bitter" that she had to go out into the lobby to pull herself together. "I feel ashamed," she once wrote of the street beggars in Shanghai, "to see men and women and not to feel kinship with them." It was a rare, possibly unique, lapse. "I do believe in the brotherhood of man, I do think that one's life is too little to give for bringing about better relationships between human beings, and I feel that there is no human being on this earth of ours, irrespective or race, creed, or nationality, who should not be included among those to be served and helped."

Jane Addams said she lived on Halsted Street because it was the most interesting part of Chicago, and Lillian Wald found beauty as well as squalor on the East Side, to say nothing of the courage and goodness and devotion of many of the people who lived there. To her the spans of the great bridges and their towers that could be seen from a point near the house on Henry Street were "as magnificent if not as storied as the bridges of London and Paris," and when the sun set behind "the lofty Woolworth tower" and "the roofs and masses of the Municipal Buildings," the "glory of the Lord" seemed to rest over them. In an article she wrote in 1932 on "What Keeps the Nurses Going?" she answered her own question thus: "There is a lift . . . in the job itself that helps carry the nurse along. Her work is never a monotonous round. She can count on change, variety, plenty of 'human interest' in her day."[6]

IV

The supreme expression of Lillian Wald's personality was achieved in the way the work of the Henry Street settlement developed. Everything "came" as Keats said poetry should come, as naturally, as inevitably as leaves to a tree. As we have seen, her basic idea embraced only nursing, and it was as simple as it was original. Visiting nurses, affiliated with no particular religious or secular body, would go into the homes to take care of people who were not sick enough to be taken to the hospital or who could not pay for hospital care even if they were, and no distinction would be made between those who could pay for such services and those who could not. Nor was the basic idea ever abandoned. It simply expanded.

The filth and disease that Lillian Wald and her nurses encountered when they began their work are nauseating even to read about. The risk of contamination was of course very great; one wonders sometimes how any of the pioneers managed to survive. But they would have had to be something worse than fools if, having relieved a particular patient, they had not raised any question as to what had produced his sickness or what, if anything, could be done to prevent reinfection or the same condition in others. Sometimes the nurse herself worked like a charwoman, but that was only a beginning. Having taken care of this particular case, how could she go away without trying to teach the well-meaning but ignorant, often foreign, housewife, herded into the ghetto, untaught in the ways of American cities, and sometimes unable even to communicate with those who might have helped her, that survival itself must depend for her family upon "cleanliness, personal hygiene, temperance, and good cooking"? How, in other words, could she avoid undertaking an educational as well as, in the narrower sense, a healing work?

That in itself was hard enough, but it was not possible to stop there, for even slum homes were not islands. Here was a boy with an infected scalp, who, since there were as yet no school nurses, was simply told to go home every time he appeared at school but whom nobody restrained from playing with well children in the street and infecting them there. What could be done about that without setting up school nurses to treat him and put him back in school and keep him from contaminating others? Here was a retarded or otherwise handicapped child who could not keep up with his class. Must he fall by the wayside or grow up a delinquent and an expensive charge upon society, or should "ungraded" schools be established to teach him whatever he may be capable of learning at whatever rate he is able to travel? Here was a tenement where children's clothing was being made in close proximity to sixteen cases of measles, while a tuberculosis patient was sitting up in bed, coughing, making cigarettes for the market, and moistening the paper with her lips. How could you deal with that without getting involved in legislation? One does not need to be what would later be called a "bleeding-heart liberal" to be able to understand that these were not debatable questions upon which good men might differ. Intelligent selfishness, to be sure, would be quite capable of dealing with all of them, except that selfishness alone is never intelligent, for Dante's definition of the damned as those who have lost the good of the understanding is still the greatest that has ever been framed.

Policemen on the East Side got into the habit of telling people that "there's a lady over on Henry Street who might help you." No doubt there were those who thought Lillian Wald should have "stuck" to her nursing. She wrote of Dr. Jacobi that "he frequently pointed out the fundamental relationship to health of suitable hours, suitable working conditions and other factors," and looking back over her own life, she once said that she was startled when the realization came to her that when she thought she was only working in the interest of the East Side babies, she was really in politics. By 1929 she was working for the removal of outdoor privies, a separate toilet for every tenement family, better fire protection, and the abolition of cellar dwellings and apartments with no window openings.

But Lillian Wald would not have been herself if she had not realized that people have more than physical needs and that there is not much point in saving a life if the life that is saved is not going to be worth living. Sick little girls were sometimes brought flowers and dolls as well as medicine; indeed, such things *were* medicine. The romanticized Horatio Alger conception of the newsboy did not attract Lillian Wald because she knew how close the connection was between street life and delinquency, but she never overlooked the importance of play in the child's growing into life. The "Bunker Hill" pioneering playground for children was on the Henry Street grounds, and in 1902, under Mayor Seth Low, the city set up the Seward Park municipal playground.

The most impressive work of the Henry Street settlement in the arts came with the work of Alice and Irene Lewisohn at what became the famous Neighborhood Playhouse, an institution in the cultural life of the city. There were performed such plays as *The Dybbuk*, *The Little Clay Cart*, Galsworthy's *The Mob*, and *The Shepherd*, by Olive Tilford Dargan. Yvette Guilbert came to appear in the French miracle play *Gibour*; Ellen Terry read from Shakespeare and Mrs. LeMoyne from Browning. But there were other things that, in a different way, were quite as important. Lillian Wald, like Jane Addams, knew that you cannot get rid of "gangs" without giving boys other kinds of organized fellowship in which the energies that "gangs" release destructively can be turned to constructive use, and Clinton Hall was opened in 1904 to provide a place for dances that were not just an excuse for drinking in halls supplied by the liquor interests and operated for their profit.

If there were those who thought the nurses should "stick"

to their nursing, there were many others who saw the logic of settlement-house workers interesting themselves in juvenile court legislation, the prevention of cruelty to children, or even child labor laws, but who were still inclined to insist that they must stop there. These people were perhaps a little more humane than the first group but they were hardly more intelligent nor did they understand the network of interdependence which embraces us all in modern society. When a young woman called at Henry Street, one evening in the nineties, in search of help in organizing a trade union, Lillian Wald was not even familiar with the term, but by 1903 she was being invited to share in the formation of the National Women's Trades Union League. In 1911 the settlement was involved in the protests which sparked new legislation after 143 lives had been lost in a fire at the Triangle Waist Company because the doors had been locked to make it easier for the employers to check on petty thievery, and in 1913 the settlement supported the famous textile workers' strike in Lawrence, Massachusetts.

The settlement reached out in all directions, both at home and abroad. One Sunday night supper at Henry Street was attended by Theodore Roosevelt, Jacob Riis, William Dean Howells, Richard Watson Gilder, Felix Adler, Seth Low, and others. Young women came from China in search of instruction in public-health nursing from Lillian Wald. Like many of their Russian Jewish neighbors, Henry Street became interested in revolutionary activity in Russia early in the century, and Prince Peter Kropotkin and the beloved "Babuschka" (Katharine Breshkovsky, "the Little Grandmother of the Russian Revolution") were welcome friends at the settlement. Lillian Wald helped persuade President Roosevelt to refuse the request of the czar's government for the extradition of one refugee and encouraged the American Friends of Russian Freedom in its efforts to free other political prisoners. When the revolution finally materialized, however, "Babuschka" did not like it. She had wanted democracy, and what she got was a totalitarian dictatorship. Lillian Wald understood her attitude and she herself recognized all the shortcomings of the Soviet regime, but she refused to join the red baiters or see no good in Soviet Russia.

In 1924 she visited there by invitation to consult on problems involving public health and child welfare,[7] and she favored American recognition of the new regime long before FDR brought it about. "Without touching upon the political significance, it seems to me unthinkable that where there is so much in common, so many interests and aspirations, we should continue the present awkward relationship by refusing to acknowledge formally the obvious fact of a responsible government in Russia."

Prohibition she supported clear to the end of the chapter, unimpressed by the argument that it had been "put over" upon the people under the influence of war and postwar emotionalism. "At the time the Eighteenth Amendment went into effect, on January 16, 1920, two thirds of the states had already adopted prohibition by popular vote, about 90 per cent of the land area was at least theoretically dry, and nearly 70 per cent of the American people nominally lived under a dry regime." She was not under the impression that prohibition had created a utopia; neither had she expected it to do so. But she did know that the liquor interests had always been lawless and a force toward political corruption, that excessive drinking and promiscuity among young people did not begin with prohibition, and, above all, that her neighbors were far better off now than they had been before. Under prohibition alcoholism declined notably on the East Side; drunkenness ceased to be a factor in most charity cases; and the money that until now had been wasted on liquor was increasingly invested in what the family needed for its well-being.[8]

Lillian Wald did not expect to escape from her sponsorship of causes without paying a price. Her support of a cloakmakers' strike, her affiliation with the Progressive Party, her belief in woman suffrage—all this and much besides seemed to some supporters of Henry Street adequate reason for withholding money to cure sick babies. Lillian Wald grieved for them rather than for herself, but she knew she could build nothing on a foundation of cowardice and dishonesty, and she was proud when, in one crisis, a friend told her, "If you had taken another stand I never would have believed in another human being."

Nothing else that Lillian Wald said or did roused more antagonism than her pacifism, and by the same token there was no other front on which she could have found it harder to retreat. If war was right, then everything she had lived and worked for was wrong, for war was an evil that embraced and sanctioned and fostered all the rest. The American Union Against Militarism had one "success," for its full-page advertisement in New York City and Texas newspapers correcting the false reports that were fanning war fever at the time of Wilson's awkward and half-hearted skirmish with Mexico in the spring of 1916 may well have helped to prevent a full-scale invasion.[9] But in trying to persuade Wilson not to enter World War I, the Union failed, and we are all still living with the results of that failure. Wilson was courteous, sympathetic; he could be "deeply touched"; he did not "know what steps it will be practicable to take in the immediate future to safeguard the things which I agree with you in thinking ought in any circumstances to be safeguarded," but Lillian Wald might be sure he would "have the matter in mind." She cannot have been wholly unprepared for this, for she knew that, even in meeting social workers on their own ground, Wilson did not enter into any discussion or ask any questions that might lead to understanding. "He seemed to know superbly how to state opinions, but not how to elicit information from others." In this respect, as in so many others, Theodore Roosevelt, generally regarded as much more belligerent, was his great antithesis. Certainly Roosevelt seemed much more belligerent than Wilson in 1916; that was why Lillian Wald voted for Wilson rather than for TR's candidate, Charles Evans Hughes. She had no opportunity to clash with Roosevelt on any war-related issue, for he was not in authority in 1916, and there had been no war issue during his presidency. But when she lunched with him and the *Outlook* staff to discuss a local strike, he wanted to know all about it in every aspect—the issues, the chances for settlement, even the names of the strikers involved.

Lillian Wald was never one to cry for the moon nor to refuse half a loaf when no whole one was available. Her American Union Against Militarism was less interested in feeling noble because it had taken a "stand" or borne its "testimony" than in advocating measures which there was a reasonable chance of getting through. In the days that led up to our entrance into the war, it did not oppose the defense of American rights on the high seas nor the right of the belligerents to purchase American arms but tried rather to prevent the shipping of munitions in armed American ships. After we had entered the war, Lillian Wald served in any capacity she considered ameliorative of war's horrors, defending conscientious objectors and civil liberties, but the closest she came to supporting the war was in allowing Henry Street to be used by the draft board; not being able to prevent registration, she tried to make it as fair and as humanely administered as she could for her neighbors.

V

It must be admitted that the specifically Jewish note in Lillian Wald's work is less important than it was with Rebecca Gratz, Emma Lazarus, or Henrietta Szold. It is true that the Henry Street neighborhood was largely Jewish and that Jews were important among Lillian's financial backers, but Henry Street also knew Italians, Poles, Greeks, Germans, and blacks. Miss Wald certainly did not go to Henry Street *because* it was Jewish, and though she was conscious of her kinship, she certainly did not favor or cherish Jews above their Gentile neighbors. When, toward the end of her life, anti-Semitism flared with the rise of Hitler, she saw it as no more anti-Jewish than anti-Christian (an "insult to Jesus and His teachings"), and antihuman.[10]

All creeds [she wrote] have a common basis for fellowship, and their adherents may work together for humanity with mutual respect and esteem for the conviction of each when these are not brought into controversy. Protestants, Catholics, Jews, an occasional Buddhist, and those who can claim no creed have lived and served together in the Henry Street house contented and happy, with no attempt to impose their theological convictions upon one another or upon the members of the clubs and classes who come in confidence to us.

Anti-Semitism was not unknown, however, even on Henry Street. There was a boy who announced his intention to kill a Jewish classmate at Easter because "he killed my Gawd," and who, when reminded that Jesus was himself a Jew, admitted that he was then but declared that he was an American now. And there was the Irish woman who, having received a kindness from a Protestant neighbor, reached out for a vision of a good time to come when Catholics and Protestants could forget their "bigotry" and join forces "to wipe the Jews off the face of the earth." Lillian Wald herself thought of Christ (it is interesting that she seems generally to have referred to him thus, rather than, as one might expect from a Jew, Jesus) as one of the light-bringers, a prophet of the brotherhood of all mankind. Once, in a dream, she "watched two spirited horses pulling a great wagon along a Russian road. The wagon . . . was loaded to overflowing with crosses—rusted, bent, and broken; and when the driver turned I saw the face of Christ radiant." When she visited President Calles in Mexico, she took occasion to protest his antireligious policy by urging him to distinguish between the abuses of clericalism and religion itself.

When Jane Addams died, a Greek neighbor, visiting Hull-House, asked, "She Catholic? She Orthodox? She Jewish?" and receiving a negative reply to all these questions, suddenly reached out to grasp realization with "Oh, I see! She all religions." The same might well have been said of Lillian Wald.

Emma Goldman
1869–1940

I

WHEN I WAS a child, I used to be taken to Waldheim, one
of Chicago's West Side cemeteries,[1] in Forest Park, Illinois,
where my grandparents were buried. As a child I had such a
passion for statues that one might have supposed I was des-
tined to become a sculptor. Emma Goldman has recorded
that when she first came to America "ecstasy" took possession of her at the sight of the Statue of Liberty. But, as she
has recently revealed in her penetrating autobiography,[2]
Claire Bloom's experience, when she was sent here as a child
out of wartime England, was quite different. To her the gigantic figure suggested menace rather than welcome, and
she was half afraid Miss Liberty might be about to throw her
torch at the ship. This seems to me quite a natural reaction
on the part of a child, and perhaps I understand it better because of the way I myself felt about the anarchist monument
in Waldheim.

The "Chicago Anarchists" had been buried not far from
our family lot—August Spies, Adolph Fischer, George Engel,
and Albert R. Parsons, who were hanged on November 11,
1887, together with Louis Lingg, who had committed suicide in his cell. Two more—Samuel Fielden and Michael
Schwab—had been saved from the gallows and their sen-
tences commuted from death to prison by Governor Richard J. Oglesby the day before.

The dead men lay in a large plot, surrounded by a substantial and highly ornamental iron fence, always kept
freshly painted in red, black, and gold, under a large monument whose outstanding feature was a heroic statue of a mil-

itant appearing woman, defiantly confronting a presumably
hostile world and placing a crown of laurel upon the brow
of the prostrate martyr she shielded with her body and bil-
lowing cloak. The legend, which was from Spies, pro-
claimed: "The day will come when our silence will be more
powerful than the voices you are throttling today."

I did not know what "throttling" meant, but it sounded
very dangerous. Neither did I know then that the men buried there had been the victims of one of the most shocking
miscarriages of justice in American history. When the anarchists were hanged, my mother was eighteen years old,
and it is an indication of the hysteria which had gripped the
city that she performed an errand she had to do downtown
with considerable trepidation because it was being whis-
pered everywhere that if the executions took place, the anarchists would blow up Chicago. But Emma Goldman knew
what my mother did not know; so too did Voltairine de
Cleyre,[3] and though it would be rash to say that they both
became anarchists *because* of the executions, there can be
no doubt whatever that what happened on that black November day became one of the great formative influences in
their lives; it was suitable that both should themselves be
buried, when their time came, not far from the anarchist
monument.

The so-called Haymarket Riot was not a riot; neither did
it take place in the Haymarket. The meeting which had been
called to protest police brutality in connection with a strike
at the McCormick Reaper works was held in Desplaines
Street, just off the Haymarket, on the evening of May 4,
1886. Because the weather was threatening, it was not heavily attended. Mayor Carter H. Harrison, Sr., was present,
and when he went home, he was sure that there was nothing
to worry about. After he had left, a police captain named
John Bonfield came in literally looking for trouble, and a
bomb, thrown by an unknown hand, killed one policeman
outright and mortally wounded seven more. The next morning the *Chicago Tribune* reported that the police thereupon
drew their revolvers and fired at least 250 shots into the
crowd.

All the known radicals in Chicago were rounded up, and

after a trial so unfair that it called forth protests even from conservatives, eight men were found guilty of murder. As William Dean Howells, the only front-rank American writer of his time with the courage and decency to lay his career on the line in their behalf, afterwards pointed out,

one was at home playing cards with his family, another was addressing a meeting five miles away, another was present with his wife and little children, two others had made pacific speeches, and not one, except on the testimony of a single, notoriously untruthful witness, was proven to have anything to do with the throwing of the Haymarket bomb, or to have even remotely instigated the act. . . . Spies was convicted of murder partly because he conspired against Society with men some of whom he was not on speaking terms with . . . and the Supreme Court of Illinois, reviewing the testimony, located [Parsons] at two points, a block apart, when the bomb was thrown, and found him doubly privy to the act upon this topographical conceit.

What distressed Howells most was that his country had betrayed herself and that "this free Republic has killed five men for their opinions."

The execution of the anarchists turned generous young people like Emma Goldman and Voltairine de Cleyre toward radicalism, but through the terror it awakened in the unthinking, it set back the cause of labor in the United States for nobody knows how many years. It also inspired one act of political heroism, whose memory, as Shakespeare might say, still shines "like a good deed in a naughty world." When John Peter Altgeld was elected governor of Illinois in 1892, Fielden, Schwab, and Oscar Neebe were still in prison. Altgeld commenced an investigation, vowing that once he had decided these men were innocent, they would not remain there one day longer, no matter what the cost to himself. The next year he pardoned them, and not content with that, issued a statement in which he virtually indicted the community for judicial murder. I know of no other political leader who deliberately committed political suicide for conscience' sake at the height of his career. In spite of the hysteria which ensued, there were many (I am proud to remember that my father, faithful Republican though he was, was one of them) who knew that the uproar was all nonsense. When

Altgeld died in 1902 and his body lay in state in the Chicago Public Library, 50,000 people lined up on Michigan Avenue in a cold March wind blowing in off the lake so that they might look for the last time upon the face of the man whom the newspapers had described as the Nero of the nineteenth century. Yet as late as the time young Vachel Lindsay wrote his memorial tribute to Altgeld, he could still call it appropriately "The Eagle That Is Forgotten."[4]

II

Emma Goldman was only five feet tall, but she had a jaw like a bulldog, and in Theodore Roosevelt's time, most "right-thinking" Americans (including TR) regarded her as a kind of female red devil. Frank Harris, who admired her, thought her "clearly not for ornament" and told her that her hat looked as if it had been stuffed into her pocket[5] (in those days, it seems, a sufficiently radical lady might make shift to get along without her marriage lines, but she could not be expected to dispense with her hat). She had a sharp tongue, and she could be brusque and overbearing. She horse-whipped her former mentor Johann Most in public after he had repudiated Alexander Berkman, and when a police officer promised to quash the charges against her if she would turn informer, she threw a glass of water into his face. "The more opposition I encountered, the more I was in my element," she says, "and the more caustic I became with my opponents."

Yet, just as her phenomenal energy coexisted with a number of serious ailments, including, at one period, tuberculosis, so her combativeness kept house with a great tenderness. Margaret Anderson of the *Little Review* remembered her as "gay, communicative, tender" and has recorded that, on the beach at night, she sang Russian folk songs "in a low and husky voice," and it would be hard to surpass the patient loving-kindness she displays in her letters. In one of her brushes with the law, the prosecutor found it necessary to admonish the jury that the "well-bred lady, courteous, and with a pleasant smile on her face," was not "the real Emma Goldman" whom it was their duty to convict, or, in other words, that they must blot out the actual woman before them and replace her with his mental image of her! Other hostile witnesses described her as "a woman of great ability and of personal magnetism" and "a very able and intelligent woman and a fine speaker." Samuel Eliot Morison said she was about the finest woman speaker he ever heard, and John Dewey called her "a romantically idealistic person with a highly attractive personality."

She was a nurse who never refused a case whatever the nature of the disease nor the patient's attitude toward her. "Every rise in the temperature of my charges used to alarm me, and a death would upset me for weeks. In all my years of nursing I had never learned detachment or indifference to suffering." Even when she was living on the edge of destitution herself, she would divide whatever she had with anybody who needed it. No degradation in those she tried to help repelled her; in the Jefferson City prison, she found no one that was "depraved, cruel, or hard," and I do not know where she shows her real delicacy of feeling better than in her inability to ask anybody for what offense she had been sent up. Said a newspaper woman of wide acquaintance: "I never met anybody who had had any contact with her who did not swear by her."

Emma Goldman was born into a Jewish family at Kovno, Russia (later known as Kaunas in Lithuania), on June 27, 1869. She had two older half-sisters and two younger brothers. She also had blonde hair and blue eyes; her unsympathetic and sometimes brutal father, who had wanted a son, said her eyes and hair must have come from the pig's market. He was a small shopkeeper and later, after the family had moved to Popelan in Kurland Province, near the Russ-German border, an innkeeper. Emma's mother had loved her first husband, but her marriage to Abraham Goldman had been "arranged" in the orthodox Jewish fashion, and she apparently cared comparatively little for either him or her daughter; it was not until much later in her life that the latter achieved anything like a satisfying relationship with either parent. The inn was a rude place, often filled with drunken, quarrelsome men, where the child also witnessed much brutality on the part of the government agents.

At eight she was sent to school in Königsberg, where she lived with a grandmother and an uncle who abused her. The teacher of religion was cruel and the geography teacher lustful, but the German teacher became her friend, introducing her to German and French literature and taking her to the opera; at this period all her tastes were Germanic, and she devoured the romances of E. P. Marlitt with relish. She passed her examinations for the Gymnasium with credit, but the teacher of religion refused her a character recommendation. By this time her family was living in the St. Petersburg ghetto, which was swarming with refugees and brooded over by fears and reports of pogroms; here Abraham Goldman now kept a small grocery store. Emma helped support the family, first by doing knitting at home, then by working in a glove factory and a corset factory. She was now reading Russian novels and radical literature and was inspired to take Vera Pavlovna in Nicolai Chernyshevsky's *What Is To Be Done?* (1863) as a kind of model for her life.

Her sister Lena was the first member of the family to emigrate to Rochester, New York, and in 1885 Emma and Helena followed her there. Emma put in a grueling work week in a clothing factory at $2.50, which left her with only forty cents after paying for her room, board, and carfare. In 1886 the sisters were joined by the rest of the family.

In February Emma Goldman was married to Jacob Kersner but immediately found that he was impotent. She left him and to please her parents went through the process of orthodox divorce to get rid of him; then, because he threatened suicide, she remarried him, but in August 1889 she left him for good and, armed with her sewing machine, three addresses, and five dollars, went alone to New York City.

Here she promptly met Alexander Berkman, who would become the most important of the many men in her life, and the well-known agitator-editor of *Freiheit*, Johann Most, who set to work to make a speaker of her. The next year she undertook her first brief speaking tour. At first she lectured in Russian, German, and Yiddish; later she switched to English. She became involved in the strike called by the newly formed Cloakmakers Union, and she was prominent in the anarchist May Day demonstration of 1891.

In 1892 she conspired with Berkman in his abortive attempt to kill Henry Clay Frick for his conduct in connection with the disastrous strike at the Carnegie plant in Homestead, Pennsylvania. With Carnegie himself conveniently absent, Frick's behavior had been high-handed in the extreme; he had practically employed a private army, and bloodshed had resulted. Both Benjamin Harrison and the *New York Tribune* thought the GOP lost the fall election because of Homestead, but though public sympathy had been running strongly in favor of the workers, Berkman's violence and his victim's heroic fortitude under attack notably, though illogically, alienated sympathy. Since Frick did not die, the maximum sentence for Berkman's offense provided by Pennsylvania law was seven years, but he was tried on separate counts, without advice of counsel, and sentenced, through legal technicalities, to twenty-two years, of which he served fourteen. In 1893 Emma herself was sent for a year to Blackwell's Island because, bolstering her case by quoting Cardinal Manning, she had told a Union Square audience that it was their "sacred right" to take bread if they were hungry and it was not given to them.

This turned out to be a very fortunate incarceration. Assigned at first to the sewing shop, Emma soon became a prison nurse and promptly discovered that she possessed a taste and an aptitude for this work. In 1895–96 she studied midwifery and nursing at the Allgemeines Krankenhaus in Vienna; during this time she also met prominent European anarchists and did some lecturing in England and Scotland. Having returned to Vienna in 1899, she failed to follow through to qualify herself for an M.D., but nursing proved thereafter an important means of livelihood; at one time she also operated a photographer's studio and again, with Berkman, and with characteristic generosity, an ice-cream parlor in Worcester, Massachusetts.[6]

Returning to America, she became widely known as an agitator, with neither the wolf nor the police ever very far from her door. Perhaps her worst period came after the assassination of President McKinley in 1901, when an insane attempt was made to connect her with Leon Czolgosz, with whom she had had nothing to do. Her father found himself dropped from the synagogue in Worcester, and there was a time when she went underground as "Miss E. G. Smith." Her lecturing never became wholly peaceful, however, even when she discussed literary subjects. She was often arrested and sometimes abused. Authorities denied her admission to the hall where it had been announced she would speak or dismissed the audience that had come to hear her. She said that for twenty years she never knew until the last minute whether her meeting would take place as scheduled or whether she would be dragged off the platform to jail. During one month the police stopped her in eleven places, yet during 1910 she was able to lecture 120 times before large audiences in thirty-seven cities, located in twenty-five states. In 1916, however, she was sent to jail for fifteen days for passing out birth control information.[7]

She spoke out against the Spanish-American War; much later she defended Tom Mooney when he was being railroaded to the gallows under an accusation of having bombed the Preparedness Day Parade in San Francisco, a charge which had been so flagrantly "framed" that President Wilson persistently and successfully intervened to save him. From 1906 to 1917 she edited and published a monthly magazine, *Mother Earth*, which was suppressed when, under the spell of World War I hysteria, culminating in Attorney-General Palmer's notorious "red" raids, both she and Berkman were arrested and sentenced to two years imprisonment, she at Jefferson City, Missouri, and he at Atlanta, for conspiracy to obstruct the draft.[8] Upon their release they were deported to Russia, an act which had been prepared for through the denaturalization, on very shaky legal grounds, of the missing Jacob Kersner (by her marriage to whom Emma had become an American citizen). It was eminently suitable that the then-fledgling J. Edgar Hoover should have been prominently involved in these unsavory procedures.

And then of course came the terrible anticlimax. It was in Russia that the miracle had occurred. There, in the unlikeliest place on earth, the revolution that every radical in the world had been longing for had at last been realized and utopia established. The two exiles fought their growing disillusionment for two years, but when, in 1921, the government shelled the city of Kronstadt, killing 18,000 people and crushing the last hope of the kind of community control that anarchists believed in, they ceased resisting the conviction that one tyranny had merely replaced another. The important point here is not whether they were right or wrong in this conviction but rather that when they came to the West to express it, not only all the radicals but even many liberals turned against them, and they found themselves as much abused by their erstwhile sympathizers as they had been all their lives by the conservatives.[9] Now literally a stranger and pilgrim who was wanted nowhere on earth, Emma tarried briefly in Sweden, Germany, and elsewhere; in 1925 she secured British citizenship by accepting for convenience' sake an offer of marriage from a Welsh collier, James Colton. Thereafter she lived in Canada, at St. Tropez in France, and in Loyalist Spain. In 1927 the execution of Sacco and Vanzetti revived for her all the agonies of the Chicago anarchists. It was forty years ago all over again, she told Berkman, but it was much worse now. Then she had had her life before her, with her course to choose. Now she had nothing save the crushing realization of how little all she had tried to do through all the weary years had availed.

In 1931 Alfred A. Knopf published her thousand-page autobiography, *Living My Life*, upon which he had made her an advance of $7,000. (Theodore Dreiser is said to have urged her to leave a record of the richest life of any woman of the century.) It was well received and surprisingly well reviewed even in conservative papers,[10] but the $7.50 price tag cut down sales in a depression year, as she had foretold. Though it may seem a strange thing to say, Emma Goldman had been thoroughly Americanized, and despite all she had suffered here, she loved America and believed in it above any other nation, and it hurt her to be barred from the country. In 1934 she was granted permission to return for a ninety-day lecture tour, which, however, she judged a "flop" everywhere except in Chicago. In 1936 she was saddened by the death of Alexander Berkman. Though he had fought a heroic fight and survived terrible hardships, his courage had finally been destroyed by pain and sickness, and he committed a horrible, messy suicide, which was as badly botched as his attempt to kill Frick had been. In February 1940, while working in Canada to raise money for the Spanish Loyalists, Emma suffered a stroke and died at Toronto on May 14.

III

Since most Americans in Emma Goldman's time cherished a mental image of her as a woman with a bomb in one hand and an incendiary torch in the other, it may be well to remind ourselves at the outset of our inquiry into what she really did believe and advocate that, since the heart of anarchism is its rejection of the violence which maintains the state, there is no necessary nor even natural connection between anarchist beliefs and terrorism. The conservative *New York Sun* did Emma Goldman full justice on this score: "The popular belief is that she preaches bombs and murder, but she certainly does nothing of the kind. Bombs are very definite things, and one of the peculiarities of her doctrine is its vagueness. The wonder is that with a doctrine so vague she managed to strike terror into the stout hearts of the police." And on this point the anarchist Voltairine de Cleyre was in complete agreement with the *Sun*: "I have never liked Emma Goldman or her speeches. I don't like fishwifery or billingsgate, but I never heard her say, nor any one of all I ever knew heard her, that any one could do any good by killing."

It is true nevertheless that the anarchists themselves were at least partly responsible for the identification of their movement in the public mind with violence and terror. Their agitation was at its height during the last decades of the nineteenth century, when it has been estimated by not unfriendly writers that Chicago alone had 3,000 anarchists; the year 1892 witnessed more than 1,000 dynamitings in Europe and almost 500 in America. Such actions as that of Berkman against Frick were called by the Germans an *At-*

tentat, a suicidal and self-sacrificing protest against oppressors, and Berkman himself fully expected to be required to pay for his act with his life.

It is often said that the difference between socialists and anarchists is that the socialists want the state to control everything while the anarchists want no government at all. This is not strictly accurate. It is true that Emma Goldman saw the state as itself "the coldest, most inhuman monopolist" and feared that "if once economic dictatorship were added to the already supreme political power of the State, its iron heel would cut deeper into the flesh of labor than that of capitalism today." It is also true that socialists accept trade unionism and political action as means to overthrow the capitalistic system, while anarchists regard such things as mere tinkering with the social organism; neither will they accept the dictatorship of the proletariat as an intermediate stage between revolution and the complete freedom and equality which is the ultimate or professed aim of all communists, whatever particular label they may wear. Voltairine de Cleyre stated the point at issue between anarchists and socialists perfectly: "Liberty is not the daughter but the mother of order."

What is not true is that anarchists contemplate social chaos, with no check whatever upon the actions of individuals. Those who cannot share Emma Goldman's faith in human nature may well feel that this would be the condition that would actually exist under anarchism, but it is not the end contemplated or sought. Anarchists themselves see the society that would develop in terms of voluntary cooperation on the part of various productive groups. People who do the same kind of work would form communities or collectives to work together and look after their common interests, and through this reliance upon solidarity and cooperation, a new society based upon the principle "to each according to his need, from each according to his ability" would come into being.

Anarchists in general are vague as to how all this is to be brought about, and Emma Goldman was among the vaguest. Once at least she begged the whole question of method by declaring, "I am really too much of an anarchist to work out a program for the members of that society, in fact I do not bother about all the trifling details, all I want is freedom, perfect, unrestricted liberty for myself and others." At the Amsterdam Anarchist Conference of 1907 she did commit herself to the extent of maintaining that anarchism must embrace both federalism and individualism, but her emphasis always falls on the second aspect. This was partly a matter of conviction on her part; like W. H. Auden, she wished to be delivered from "the prepared response." "Finalities," she says, "are for gods and governments, not for the human intellect." And again, "I hold that when it is said of a man that he has arrived, it means that he is finished —his development has stopped at that point. I have always striven to arrive at a state of flux and continued growth, and not to petrify in a niche of self-satisfaction." But it was much more a matter of temperament. She really had very little interest in theory, and intelligent though she was, she was not an independent thinker.

This is what Hutchins Hapgood meant when he called her more revolutionist than anarchist: "although I always greatly admired her on account of her courage and devotion, I was never interested in her thinking. Even her faith was expressed in echoes of far more creative minds, and therefore was never convincing to me." The real service she performed was, he thought, a distinctly kindly, loving, human service, "that of removing despair from those who would otherwise be hopeless. Those who would otherwise regard themselves as outcasts, after Emma, often felt a new hope and thought better about themselves." Charles A. Madison writes in the same vein: "Her strongest attribute was of an emotional rather than intellectual nature; she felt first and thought afterwards. She had an extraordinary capacity for believing whatever suited her ideological or personal purposes." He did not find it surprising that writing should have been agony for such a woman and her essays consequently much less effective than her fiery speeches. "In cold print . . . her lectures reveal little of her dynamic appeal. They are primarily the work of a forceful agitator: clear, pointed, spirited, but without originality or intellectual vigor." Henry F. May is in substantial agreement with both

Hapgood and Madison: "Utterly brave, widely compassionate, she was at her best (among prisoners for instance) a great woman, though a thoroughly shallow thinker."[11]

What it all boils down to is that hers was basically an emotional, a romantic, even, as we shall see later, though it would distress her to hear it, a religious approach, but none of these terms is employed pejoratively here. Scientific sociology, as we understand it today, was as foreign to her as what she found in Soviet Russia, where she saw the Bolsheviki as "the Jesuits of socialism," surpassing "the autocracy of the Inquisition." Nor should anybody be surprised that, since she opposed all nationalism, she was anti-Zionist. As she saw it, the greatness of the Jews was due to the very fact that they were not "divided through boundaries and blinded by their nationalistic viewpoints." If they were to have a country of their own, she was sure they would behave as badly as anybody else.[12] A perspicacious writer in the *Madison* (Wis.) *Capital Times* discerned all this in 1934, when everybody else was denouncing this dangerous woman; she stood "opposed," he observed, "to the annihilation of the individual spirit whether the massacre proceeded from Mussolini or Marx."

IV

Humanity in personal relationships is fortunately not dependent upon a romantic temperament; Shaw had a point when he spoke of the soft, cruel hearts and the hard, kind ones, but perhaps we should remind ourselves that in her pioneering book on the modern drama,[13] Emma Goldman found Shaw "limited, dogmatic, and set" as a propagandist and that she greatly preferred Hauptmann (he "embraces all, understands all, and portrays all, because nothing human is alien to him") and Galsworthy ("his background is life, 'that palpitating life,' which is the root of all sorrow and joy"). She believed that both liberals and radicals could be as narrow-minded, as hidebound, as dogmatic, and as overbearing as any mossback and that their children might quite as easily be constrained to rebel against their upbringing as the children of the manor.

Her charity toward the needy has already been spoken of. When she was in jail, she mothered her fellow prisoners, as Debs's colleague, the Catholic Kate Richards O'Hare, gladly testified. It never occurred to Emma to wonder whether anybody shared her "ideas" or had any ideas of her own; if she needed help, no other consideration was of any moment. "The Emma Goldman that I knew is not the Propagandist," wrote Mrs. O'Hare. "It is Emma Goldman, the tender, cosmic mother, the wise, understanding woman, the faithful sister, the loyal comrade. . . . Emma don't believe in Jesus, but she is one who makes it possible for me to grasp the spirit of Jesus." For her the purpose of anarchism was "to establish the sanctity of human life, the dignity of man, and the right of every human being to liberty and well-being," or, in other words, to everything which, as she saw it, was denied by the state, the church, and the capitalistic system. When Robert Minor told her that individual human life was not important, she called the statement "an outrage of revolutionary ethics. Individual life is important," she declared indignantly, "and should not be cheapened and degraded into a mere automaton." To her the individual was "not merely the result of heredity and environment, of cause and effect. . . . The living man cannot be defined; he is not a part of this or that; he is a whole, an individual whole, a growing, changing, yet always constant whole." And surely nothing could be more romantic or, in the larger sense, more democratic than this.

It was indeed remarkable that a woman who had so little faith in social organization should have had so much in individuals. Occasionally, to be sure, there is a flash of what we whose faith cannot match hers would call realism. Toward the end of her life she wrote, "Now I do not claim that the triumph of my ideas would eliminate all possible problems from the life of man for all time. . . . Nature and our own complexes are apt to continue to provide us with enough pain and struggle." And when she was displeased with the conduct of Lucy Parsons, the widow of one of the Haymarket martyrs, she found the root of the trouble "in people; the movement or lack of it has nothing to do with such things." But she does not strike such notes often. She comes much closer to her norm when she argues that under anarchism most men would cooperate freely, each carrying his share of the burden and not seeking an unfair advantage and that even "the occasional lazy individual" would not be a great problem; that if our present marriage laws were done away with, sexual jealousy would disappear with them; and that "it would be better for society and more beneficial to those who watch over them" simply to turn all prisoners loose than to maintain the present system of crime and punishment. She was right in everything she wrote about the shortcomings of the prevalent criminology, which creates criminals instead of curing them, and she was right too in ascribing the lack of incentive in many workers to the soulless drudgery of routine which has been imposed upon them. But what about the people who lack "the urge to create" as "the first and most impelling force in their lives," and what about the psychopathic killer or even the less dangerous chiseler who cares nothing about society but is concerned only with what he can carry away for himself? What will anarchism do with people like these? I have nowhere seen any evidence that Emma Goldman ever faced such problems. As Hutchins Hapgood says, she assumed "a race of men and women who had overcome their personal egotism in behalf of the common good," quite as she had. But such men and women are unfortunately still rare. Even Emma Goldman might have had more difficulty in being one of them if she had not been able to satisfy her ego, which was considerable, by asserting it in its full force against everything arrayed against it in a society that she despised.

Insofar as all this had an ideational background, it probably derived from the social-contract theory of government. Man in his natural state was free, with people living as families in small communities and with society not a state but an association. The state is an abstraction, not an organism, and it has been accepted only because people lack faith, seeing themselves and others as "evil, vicious, and too incompetent to know what is good for [them]." The Darwinian survival of the fittest as the determining factor in evolution repelled her as it repelled Samuel Butler and Bernard Shaw; instead she was thrilled by Kropotkin's view that cooperation as against mere strife and struggle had been an important factor, not only in human society but even in the animal kingdom, for she believed that all power corrupts, "that division and strife mean death, and that unity and co-operation advance [man's] cause, multiply his strength and further his welfare." "If the worship of authority can be discarded, co-operation will be spontaneous and inevitable, and the individual will find it his highest calling to contribute to the enrichment of social well-being."

All this is obviously much more a moral than an intellectual conviction, and the element of faith must play a very large part in it. Looking at the matter from where we stand now, we must surely conclude that those who reject it will be in the vast majority; moreover, one fears that there may be almost as high a percentage of these inside the churches as out of them. Nevertheless, H. L. Mencken did have a point when he wrote, "If you can distinguish [Emma Goldman's doctrine], even after long prayer, from the doctrines set forth in the Beatitudes, then you are a far more adept distinguisher than I am."

Mencken's reference to the Beatitudes may remind us that she never had the religious incentive to keep her going. The Christian has in a sense an easier row to hoe than hers; even when man fails, there is still God, who cannot fail. Upon what, then, did she rely? From what well did she draw her strength? She credits herself with a sense of humor and says she could not have survived without it, but I must say it does not appear prominently in her writings. I never heard her speak, and I should very much like to know whether she made any use of it on the platform, but I should greatly doubt it. There can be no question that she knew discouragement, especially as she grew older–poor, exiled, and alone. She had spent all her life chasing windmills, she said, and hardly anything had come of her efforts. She was a fool who clung to an ideal nobody cared about and she poisoned every moment of her life in the impossible task of trying to rouse people who could not be roused. Yet she kept on and on, and if her life could have been extended for another half century she would probably still be at it. Was she merely the slave of duty, who could not leave off following the gleam?

Or did she, when all was said and done, get more satisfaction out of her life of devotion and endless striving than any sybarite has ever known?

V

But how, then, does all this fit in with the use anarchists did make, from time to time, of violence? First of all, it must be understood that Emma Goldman was never involved in anything of this kind except at the beginning of her career when she assisted Berkman in his attempt upon the life of Henry Clay Frick. First they tried to make a bomb in a crowded tenement whose occupants were endangered by their attempt; the bomb being a failure, Berkman then moved against the industrialist with pistol and dagger. All this Emma almost at once regretted and she put it behind her forever, though she continued to maintain that those who committed such deeds had been constrained by iniquitous social conditions and she refused to cry out for their blood. "An act of political violence at the bottom is the culminating result of organized violence at the top." "Compared with the wholesale violence of capital and government, political acts of violence are but a drop in the ocean." It would be as reasonable to accuse Jesus of favoring prostitution because he protected the woman taken in adultery, she argued, as to believe that her defense of political criminals implied approval of the form their protest had taken. It is an established fact that on several occasions her coolness and self-control prevented riots at public meetings where the needless intrusion of the law had stupidly invited it. When the crowd was on her side, she always insisted that dissenters be heard, once even calling for a round of applause for a man who had had the courage to cast one lone vote against a measure she favored, which had otherwise been carried unanimously.

The kind of patriotism she believed in was "love of one's birthplace, the place of childhood's recollections and hopes, dreams and aspirations," the place where "in childlike naivety, we would watch the fleeting clouds, and wonder why we, too, could not run so swiftly." Her American heroes included Jefferson, Thomas Paine, Patrick Henry, Emerson and Thoreau, Whitman, the Boston abolitionists, and "that sombre giant John Brown" (who was surely violent enough, though it is possible she may not have known how violent), but not "Lincoln and his minions," who "followed only when abolition had become a practical issue, recognized as such by all." What she rejected completely was the kind of patriotism that is "artificially created and maintained through a network of lies and falsehoods" and whose essentials are "conceit, arrogance, and egotism," and with it she rejected war between nations. "The older I get the less I want to cause pain," she says. She became convinced that the violence of both Berkman and Czolgosz had accomplished nothing, and she did penance for her own horse-whipping of Johann Most.

Yet she was not, even in her final phase, an unqualified pacifist, though she wrestled with the problem at length and came out much closer to the pacifist position than most of the people who regarded her as a dangerous woman. In the end she rejected completely the doctrine that the end justifies the means, arguing, like Aldous Huxley, that since means modify, even determine, ends, the two cannot be dissociated. "To divest one's methods of ethical concepts means to sink into the depths of utter demoralization." Once she wrote a friend that the gun decides nothing at all. "Even if it accomplished what it sets out to do—which it rarely does—it brings so many evils in its way as to defeat its original aim."

Whether she also rejected class war along with war between nations I am not sure that she ever quite knew. She said, "I feel violence in whatever form never has [brought] and probably never will bring constructive results." She was no longer willing to bind the future to the skirts of the past; if no revolution had ever quite accomplished its aims, perhaps the reason for failure might be found in the means employed. "I insist if we can undergo changes in every other method of dealing with social issues we will also have to learn to change the methods of revolution. I think it can be done. If not I shall relinquish my belief in revolution."

This seems uncompromising enough. But she also knew that violent revolutions would continue to occur whether she believed in them or not and that disavowing them was a little like forswearing thunderstorms. She once wrote Berkman that she wished she could go the whole way with Tolstoy and Gandhi but could not quite achieve this. For one thing, Gandhi himself was "very much of a go-getter"; for another, he had behind him a tradition of nonviolent resistance which we do not have in the West. She went to Russia, where the czar's government had been overthrown by violence, hoping to find utopia there; later, in Spain, she thought that, for the first time in her experience anywhere, the kind of social order the anarchists believed in really had been set up, and she clung to the Loyalists until they had, as she saw it, betrayed the cause by joining forces with the communists, and even a little longer. "It's as though you had wanted a child all your life," she said, "and at last, when you had almost given up hoping, it had been given to you–only to die after it was born!" All in all, Emma Goldman seems to have borne to the pacifist ethic about the same relationship that John the Baptist bore to the Christian movement. Among those who remained outside the Kingdom, none were greater than she.

VI

But however all this may be, there can be no question that Emma Goldman's aesthetic sensibilities conspired with her warm humanity to save her from becoming the single-minded fanatic she might perhaps otherwise have been. She realized that she was "woven of many skeins, conflicting in style and texture. To the end of my days I should be torn between the yearning for a personal life and the need of giving all to my ideal." Like Henry James's revolutionary, the Princess Casamassimi–and like James himself–she knew that art and what to her was religion might sometimes conflict. Like the Shaw of *Back to Methuselah*, she could conceive the possibility of a time to come when, the present iniquitous social order having been done away with, all our needs might be satisfied at first hand by life itself, thus obviating the need for art. Nevertheless, as life now stands, beautiful things were not luxuries but necessities; the soul could not live nor life be bearable without them. "Every stimulus which quickens the imagination and raises the spirits is as necessary to life as air." She could not believe that even a cause meant "the denial of life and joy," and she insisted upon "freedom, the right to self-expression, everybody's right to beautiful, radiant things." Berkman sometimes thought she went too far in this direction, and this strain in her may well have been one reason why the much more ascetically inclined Voltairine de Cleyre could not trust her completely.

Though the glory of the Rockies, on her first trip to the Coast, impressed Emma with "the puerility of all man's efforts" and made the whole human race seem insignificant, she has comparatively little to say about either natural beauty or the plastic arts. She admired Rodin, Jacob Epstein, Jo Davidson, and others, and saw "the simple canvasses of a Millet" as "a tremendous factor for the awakening of conscious discontent." But what really spoke to her were music and the theater. Her love of opera dated back to the performance of *Il Trovatore* that she saw with her German teacher in Königsberg, and it remained with her all her life. Wagner and Beethoven became her favorite composers. In the theater, Duse, Julia Marlowe, and Mary Garden were among the artists who moved her profoundly, and she had associations with Paul Orlenoff and his Russian troupe (which included Alla Nazimova) when they came to America, as well as the Progressive Stage Society, the Chicago Little Theater, the Provincetown Players, and the Birmingham Repertory Theater. If her lectures and writings on the drama centered upon social significance, they were by no means exclusively concerned with this aspect. She praised Maeterlinck's *Monna Vanna* and Hauptmann's *The Sunken Bell*, among other things, for what seemed to her their forward-looking spirit, but this aspect alone can hardly explain her special enthusiasm for Rostand's *Chantecler*, which she hailed as the greatest achievement of the modern drama for its "philosophic depth and poetic beauty," seeing the cock himself as "the intense idealist, whose mission is light and truth" whose "great purpose in life is to dispel the night." Though she later judged *L'Aiglon* "a stupid play," it is interesting that her attitude toward Rostand should have been more sympathetic than that of the socialistically inclined

Howells. Though she was sometimes impatient with Whitman for his optimism, Richard Drinnon inclines to think her lectures on him more "interesting and penetrating" than some of her drama lectures, but it was the Russian dramatists on whom she came closest to doing really scholarly work, though the results of this study have never been published. Much as I like Eugene Walter's play, *The Easiest Way*, I must say, however, that her reference to it as "the only real drama America has so far produced" does not show much knowledge of our drama.

VII

Emma Goldman must have known that in tying up sexual freedom and atheism with her anarchist propaganda, she was rousing even more antagonism than would have been arrayed against her had she avoided these topics, but she refused to be silenced on either count because both were involved in her ideal of the free life. Her antagonism toward marriage must have begun at least as early as her fifteenth year when her father tried to marry her off to a man of his choice, and her pioneering work for birth control, which influenced Margaret Sanger, was undertaken because her contacts with the poor had shown her the devastating effects of uncontrolled fertility. After she had begun to defy the law by describing contraceptive methods in her lectures, she always took a book to these talks, so that she would have something to read in jail.

She was never what most people would call a physically attractive woman, yet she managed to acquire a considerable number of lovers in the course of her career, including, during her later years, a Swedish admirer considerably younger than she was. It is clear that she had no sympathy with the antimale bias which warped the outlook of so many feminists in her time; indeed she was not, in the ordinary sense of the term, a feminist at all, for though she saw no reason why women should not have the vote, she believed that men and women would divide politically along exactly the same lines and that therefore woman suffrage would accomplish little. Indeed she even believed that women in

her time were considerably less well informed on public issues than men, more prejudiced and sentimental, and the
chief supporters of established institutions, and therefore
she was not offended by Rostand's presentation of the
pheasant hen in *Chantecler* as "the eternal female, bewitch-
ingly beautiful, but self-centered and vain," with no desire
in her heart and mind save to possess the male. Consistently
with her anarchist beliefs, Emma Goldman dared to mention the unmentionable by defending the rights of homosex-
uals before most people were willing to grant that they had
any, but it seems clear that she did not like them nor regard
them as normal people.[14]

This is not the place to describe in detail the multitudi-
nous and iniquitous legal and economic disabilities under
which women suffered during Emma Goldman's lifetime
and especially during her early years, but we should certainly understand that all this goes far toward explaining her rebellion against conventional standards. She went considerably further than this alone would account for, however. She
believed that by making sex indecent, Puritanism had not
only condemned unmarried women to an unnatural condition which produced neurasthenia in them while it wore out
wives with incessant childbearing, but that it had also created a society which subsidized prostitution and venereal
disease. The latter complaint does not seem to have im-
proved, however, under the comparative sexual freedom
which has since been achieved, and some of the statements
inspired by Emma Goldman's revolt are unrealistic in the
extreme. Because she saw marriage as "primarily an economic arrangement, an insurance pact," she can declare
that "it is merely a question of degree" whether a woman
"sells herself to one man, in or out of marriage, or to many
men," which, to say the least, hardly shows a gift for fine dis-
tinctions. Indeed she goes even further when she declares
that "marriage and love have nothing in common; they are
as far apart as the poles, are, in fact, antagonistic to each
other," but this proves too extreme even for her, and she
qualifies it elsewhere, admitting that love and marriage can
coexist even though they often do not. "If motherhood is the
highest fulfillment of woman's nature," she asks, "what

other protection does it need save love and freedom?" and she was capable of citing the fact that "thousands of children [are] destitute and homeless" as proof that marriage does not protect the child, but surely she must have known that many of these children are bastards and that, as such, they have less protection than if they had been born on the other side of the blanket, though heaven knows many of them have little enough there.

In imitation of Sonya in *Crime and Punishment*, Emma once tried walking the streets to raise money to support Berkman's assault on Frick (a striking illustration of the truth of Oscar Wilde's observation that life imitates literature as much as literature imitates life), but found that she could not go through with it. Though their physical relations seem to have been pretty well over and done with from the time he emerged from prison, Berkman was the great love of Emma's life, and in a sense nobody could have been more "faithful" than she was to him, but it was a very special form of fidelity that she practiced, which did not exclude connections with Ed Brady, Dr. Ben Reitman (the Chicago "King of the Hobos"),[15] and others, nor did Berkman expect anything different either from her or from himself. I have no intention of explaining away Emma's sensuality. When Frank Harris called her a second Saint Paul, she objected only that Saint Paul was a Puritan, without declaring the comparison otherwise inappropriate! Nevertheless it seems clear that the demand for intellectual companionship and spiritual harmony was at least as strong in her amours as any other element. No doubt she was wise in denying herself a child, the conditions of her life being what they were, yet for all that, she may, like George Sand, have been temperamentally more mother than lover. As her letters show, she mothered Berkman in the tenderest possible way during her later years; for good measure, she even took on mothering Emmy Eckstein, with whom he was living, along with him. In a sense nobody could have been franker about her love life than Emma was in her autobiography, but she completely avoids the kind of clinical detail to which Frank Harris was given, and she was well aware of the difference and pointed it out both to him and to others. It was not modesty that restrained her but rather the fact that for her the basic reaction was not physical but psychological. Her whole being was involved in the love relationship; the "mere physical fact" was insufficient "to convey the tremendous effect it has upon human emotions and sensations." "I know myself well enough," she says, "to realize that I was not easy to live with," and there is an interesting passage in which she wonders whether the forces that denied her "permanency in love" were not "part of some passionate yearning . . . that no man could completely fulfill" or only "inherent in those who for ever reach out for the heights, for some ideal or exalted aim that excludes all else." Perhaps, she thought, only "occasional snatches of love" might be hoped for by one of her temperament and way of life, and this may well be a shrewd self-appraisal.[16]

VIII

Her religious rebellion is a rather more complicated matter. As with her sexual views and conduct, it was of course influenced by her rebellion against the establishment, but for a woman of her emotionalism, sensitiveness, and intelligence, she does seem oddly unresponsive to both the Jewish prophetic tradition and its continuation in Jesus. In her later years, at least, she celebrated Christmas, and she respected "the principle of brotherhood expounded by the agitator of Nazareth," but she seems curiously divided between the impulse to make Jesus her ally and to reject him for what she thought of as his otherworldliness. He was "a great teacher" when she wished to quote him in defending herself from charges that had been brought against her; she was sure he would be in jail if he were here, and she was glad to call herself a criminal in the sense in which he was a criminal. But the fact that she saw Christianity as hostile to social change made her even less sympathetic toward it than other religions, and she inclines to extend this hostility to Jesus himself. He "had no interest in the earth, in the pressing immediate needs of the poor and disinherited of his time." What he preached was "a sentimental mysticism, obscure and confused and lacking originality and vigor," and in one passage she even sees him cutting "a poor figure" in comparison with many other martyrs, including the Chicago anarchists! At one point these notions seem to have exercised a distorting effect upon her drama criticism. In her comments on Charles Rann Kennedy's play, *The Servant in the House*, she makes the scavenger "the real hero of the play; nay, its true and only savior," but seems unaware of the presence of the actual hero, the Christ figure, Manson.

As for later religious leaders like Huss, Calvin, and Luther, she saw them as "colossal figures," shining like "a sunrise amid the darkness" against "the omnipotence of Rome," but in their later careers both Calvin and Luther turned politician. Among her contemporaries, Tolstoy at least posed a problem for her. He was "the last true Christian" (one wonders why she thought herself an authority on this point), but though he "based his conception of human relationships on a new interpretation of the Gospels," he "was as far removed from present-day Christianity as Jesus was alien to the institutions of his time."

One cannot, however, leave the matter quite there. We have already seen that Kate O'Hare found something Christlike in Emma's care for her fellow prisoners, and the rabbi who followed her as a speaker at the Congress of Religious Philosophies began by saying that, in spite of all she had said against religion, she was the most religious person he knew. On Blackwell's Island she became friendly with a Roman Catholic priest who lent her books and discussed music with her. He never gave her a Bible until she asked for it, and when she asked him why he had waited, he told her it was because he believed nobody could learn to love the Bible until he came to it of his own desire. Thereafter "its simplicity of language and legendry" fascinated her, while as for the priest, "my own ideal, my faith, was at the opposite pole from his, but I knew he was as ardently sincere as I. Our fervor was our meeting-ground."

Insofar as religion is devotion and consecration to something greater than oneself, Emma certainly *was* religious, but her devotion was directed toward a purely human ideal. Sensitive though she was to aesthetic influences, one can only conclude therefore that mystical awareness was lacking in her and that she seems to have had no needs that could not be satisfied in terms of human relations upon the earth plane. Yet she speaks of "the human soul." The "when I come before my maker" in one letter was probably not meant to be taken literally, and I have no idea what she meant by "evidently it was not to be" in a letter to Berkman.

The interesting thing is, all this being the case, that she should still have come so close to agreement with religionists upon what orthodox Christians call conversion. It would be generally granted, I suppose, that all religions, however absurd some of their dogmas may be, do have a power to transform human life and character which seems denied to a purely ethical ideal, and the basic reason for this seems to be that the best the ethical teacher can do is to hold up a model wholly external to the sinner and say, "Thus must thou do and so," while the religionist moves unerringly to the heart of the matter, insisting that the sinner himself must be made over, identifying his will with the will of God. This is essentially what Emma Goldman does with both society and those individuals in it who must be counted upon to redeem it, and it was for this reason that she had no patience with what she considered mere social tinkering, even upon such a gigantic scale as finally emerged in Russia. "The radicals," she said, "no less than the feminists, must realize that a mere external change in their economic and political status cannot alter the inherited and acquired prejudices and superstitions which underlie their slavery and dependence, and which are the main causes of the antagonism between the sexes." And again, more comprehensively, "In my opinion . . . the great mission of revolution, of the *Social* Revolution, is a *fundamental transvaluation* of values. A transvaluation not only of social, but also of human values." That this is possible is due to the fact that "human nature is by no means a fixed quantity," but "is plastic and can be changed."

IX

If we are to judge people by their loyalty to their own principles and ideals rather than (when we differ from them) our own, it is difficult to see how any fair-minded person can withhold admiration from Emma Goldman. Not only did she labor unceasingly under threat of arrest, there were even times when she could not obtain a room in which to rest her head. At one period she snatched naps while riding through the night on the streetcars; again, she took lodgings in what she afterwards found to be a brothel. It is but simple justice to point out that there were times when the anarchists met the Christian martyrs themselves on the score of both devotion and highmindedness and accomplished this without supernatural sanctions. Voltairine de Cleyre not only refused to prosecute the man who had tried to kill her but even attempted to raise funds for his defense, and Emma herself declined to identify a policeman who had struck her in the face and knocked out a tooth.

Henry Miller called his encounter with her the most important in his life, and she was one of the great awakening influences upon Roger Baldwin, the founder of the American Civil Liberties Union. Much of her work had nothing to do with anarchism as such but merely with the defense of basic American liberties under the Bill of Rights. Moreover, as her excellent biographer Richard Drinnon observes, her "free-speech fights were ultimately successful in a remarkable number of places." She spent her life on sentry duty, as a watch dog for liberty, and wherever oppression raised its head, she rushed into the fray, whether there was any reasonable hope of success or not. As she herself said, there was a "still voice" in her which would not be silenced "and which wants to cry out against the wretchedness and injustice of the world."

Henrietta Szold

1860–1945

I

DURING ONE OF the telecasts he made during his presidency, Richard Nixon remarked that he could not "help" his face. Like many of his statements, this one did not meet with universal acceptance. By the time he has reached middle age, it was argued, every man has had a large and important share in making his face.

If one may judge by her photographs, Henrietta Szold was not a pretty girl or young woman. Her later portraits are quite different. If she is still not "pretty," she is something better. She is beautiful. Her face has become the mirror of a radiant spirit, developed through a long life of loving and unselfish service to her own people and to all mankind. One might have said of her what Lyman Abbott said of the aged Whittier, who reminded him of Moses after his descent from the mount, when his face shone.

She was born in Baltimore on December 21, 1860, the eldest daughter of the Reverend Dr. Benjamin Szold, rabbi of the Oheb Shalom Synagogue, and his wife, Sophia Schaar Szold, both of Hungarian descent.[1] Benjamin Szold became a political exile after having taken part in the revolution of 1848 and was called to America by the Baltimore congregation after his marriage in 1859. Henrietta was the eldest of eight daughters, of whom two died in infancy, another at the age of four, and still another in her twenties. There were no sons. Rachel was married to the psychologist Joseph Jastrow; Adele, the youngest and the rebel of the family, much less happily, to the publisher Thomas Seltzer; Bertha to Louis H. Levin, with whom she had five children.

She was the only one of the Szold sisters to outlive Henrietta and the only one to leave issue.

Henrietta's earliest recollection was the sight of a group of women preparing bandages for soldiers, and she also remembered her mother's pointing out to her the auction block at the intersection of Eutaw and Camden streets from which slaves had been sold. At four she witnessed the funeral procession of Abraham Lincoln as it passed through Baltimore, with her father, along with other prominent clergymen of the city, marching in it. Jeffersonian in his political philosophy, Rabbi Szold had stood behind Lincoln in his insistence upon the preservation of the Union and had once appealed to him personally in behalf of a deserter. Lincoln passed the buck to General Meade, who proved unresponsive, and Szold stayed with the offender to the bloody end.

A moderate by temperament, Dr. Szold did not see eye to eye with his orthodox brethren at all points, but neither did he join with the reform movement being headed by Isaac M. Wise and the Hebrew Union College in Cincinnati, his position being rather that of what is now known as conservative Judaism. He treated Henrietta more like a son than a daughter, encouraging her to study the Torah and the Talmud and making her not only his amanuensis but his assistant and almost his collaborator in all his scholarly work. After his death, it was she who went daily to the synagogue to say the Kaddish for him, the office customarily performed by the eldest son or, such issue failing, by a male kinsman as a substitute for him. Even when she was a small child, her father would not make Henrietta's decisions for her; instead he would analyze the problem for her and leave the result to her own best judgment.

Nevertheless it is possible that her closeness to her father and her sense of his dependence upon her may have been a factor in preventing her from going to college, for though a college education for girls was unusual in those days, Henrietta's younger sisters did manage to get some. It may also, unintentionally, have prevented her from forming fruitful relationships with young men that might have led to marriage. In later life she said that though she might have missed the pleasures of youth, she was going to insist on the privileges of old age, but she can hardly be said to have done this when she kept herself chained to a grueling job in Palestine when she was longing for home. Rabbi Szold died in 1902, after Henrietta and her mother had nursed him through a long and painful illness, but as long as she lived she kept asking herself what he would have thought of this or that problem and what he would have done about it. Moreover, even in her life of service and high accomplishment, she was always a little uneasy, feeling that she had not fulfilled the hopes her father had entertained for her as a scholar.

She attended the public schools of Baltimore and graduated at the head of her class and as a commencement speaker from the Western Female High School in 1877. She also studied in the religious school of her father's synagogue and privately with him. German was spoken in the home, and, as late as Hitler's time, she was urging the German exiles in Palestine not to allow themselves to forget their native tongue. By now good judges had testified that they had never detected a mistake in her spoken Hebrew, but it took her a long time to feel really at home with that language, if indeed she ever did. Her father was a good classicist as well as a Hebrew scholar. She learned French also, and she seems to have had enough Italian to make herself understood in Italy. Once, as a girl, she complied with Morris Jastrow's request to write a letter for him in French to Sarah Bernhardt, asking for her autograph, but the great lady did not deliver.

After her graduation from high school, Henrietta Szold was asked to substitute briefly as both teacher of English and (amazingly) principal; from here she went shortly to the Misses Adams' School for Girls, where she remained for many years, teaching almost everything in the curriculum at the magnificent salary of fifteen dollars a month. She also taught in the religious school at the synagogue, and, as "Sulamith," began writing extensively for the *Jewish Messenger*.

She afterwards felt that she had been a good deal of a humbug as a teacher, and she soon discovered that her views about teaching were far ahead of her time. To her way of thinking, education was something more than either stuffing the child's mind with facts or preparing him to earn a living. It was a matter of opening blind eyes and unstopping deaf ears, developing his whole personality, and preparing him for life in the twentieth century, which, she already sensed, was not going to be easy. Science too was more important in her thinking than it was in most people's at the time, "because observation precedes even language, language presupposes observation." As for literature, especially poetry, it should be taught for its beauty, its life values, and its appeal to the imagination, and not as something which provided opportunities for parsing. When she delivered an address in which such views as these were expressed before the Maryland State Teachers' Association, at Old Point Comfort, Virginia, she did not feel that she had received a warm reception. Nor, for her part, did she feel any desire to be like most of the teachers she encountered there.

Her teaching as well as her organizational and executive ability were soon to be tested in another theater. We have already observed in connection with the work of Emma Lazarus how eastern European Jews began pouring into eastern American cities as they fled from the pogroms of the 1880s. In Baltimore, as Marvin Lowenthal has phrased it, the Szold home became for these refugees "a confessional, a wailing wall, a free boarding house, and an unofficial one-man employment bureau," and in 1889 Henrietta Szold opened one of the pioneer night schools to teach "English, English, and again English," killing considerably more than one bird with a single stone by using Edward Eggleston's *History of the United States* as a textbook in "history, geography, grammar, spelling, writing, and conversation." The problems were those one might have expected from a student body in which boys and girls and older men and women in every stage of education sat side by side, but though the school began with thirty pupils, it had handled 5,000 and served as a model for other schools elsewhere before the project was given up in 1898. (She had resigned as superintendent in 1893).[2]

In that same year, she had become editorial secretary of the Jewish Publication Society of America (founded, 1888), a position which necessitated residence for a time in Philadelphia, and which she held until 1915 (Louis Lipsky says that, except for directors and canvassers, she *was* the society). Its purpose was to make the Jewish classics available in English and to publish important new books on Jewish subjects. Miss Szold's position involved endless drudgery in the way of editing, proofreading, translating and sometimes rewriting, and index-making, and among the works which passed through her hands were Heinrich Graetz's great *History of the Jews*, Louis Ginzberg's *The Legends of the Jews*, and Morris Lazarus's *The Ethics of Judaism*, to say nothing of her work on *The American Jewish Year Book* from its establishment in 1889, and as its sole editor from 1904 to 1908. She also indexed the publications of the American Jewish Historical Society, contributed fifteen articles to *The Jewish Encyclopaedia*, and gave numerous lectures, including two before the World's Parliament of Religions at the World's Columbian Exposition in Chicago in 1893.

In 1903, the year after her father's death, she moved with her mother to New York, where she attended classes at the Jewish Theological Seminary in the hope of acquiring sufficient scholarship to edit her father's manuscripts. This she never accomplished, being deflected by other duties and perhaps also by her relationship to Louis Ginzberg, a German professor in the seminary, to whom, in the then state of his knowledge of English, her services became as important as they had been in other ways to her father, and with whom, though he was thirteen years her junior, she fell hopelessly and obsessively in love.[3]

Their acquaintance began in February 1903, and it was not until the fall of 1908 that, after some cryptic and mysterious letters, he returned from Europe to tell his friend that he was engaged to Adele Katzenstein, a beautiful girl with whom he had fallen in love, virtually at first sight, upon glimpsing her in a Berlin synagogue. On November 17, 1908, Henrietta wrote, "Today it is four weeks since my only real happiness was killed," and it took her a long time to get over it; indeed she continued what she seems to have regarded as the self-therapy of her diary entries until July 20, 1910. She had been to Europe once before with her father in 1881; now, on July 30, 1909, she sailed again, this time with her mother, for a trip which would also embrace Palestine and play an important part in determining the direction of her work and her destiny for the rest of her days. Ginzberg and Adele Katzenstein were married in London in May 1909.

At this distance of time it is neither necessary nor possible to determine the rights and wrongs of so painful an experience, but Eli Ginzberg's biography seems to dispose of his father's statement, as reported by Irving Fineman, that he had never remotely suspected Miss Szold's feelings for him. At the very least it must be said that he was not bashful about incurring obligations to her, and when their break came, he seems to have shown more interest in holding himself free of all blame than of sympathizing with her position. At his request, Henrietta wrote Adele a beautiful letter,[4] but the hope expressed in it that the two women might become close friends was not realized, and when, early in 1909, "Very truly yours, Louis Ginzberg" wrote to "Dear Miss Szold" for permission to include her name in the preface to one of his books, she apparently refused. Eli Ginzberg also records that it became a stock joke in their family to describe Louis Ginzberg as "the father of Hadassah," and surely it was a singularly tasteless one. The two last saw each other in Jerusalem in 1934. There is a weird and wry footnote to the whole story in the fact that after Henrietta's death, Eli himself married one of her cousins.

What she saw of the sanitary conditions under which people were living in Palestine in 1909 was so terrible that it made any purely personal woes seem insignificant in comparison. She had joined the Zionist Association of Baltimore as early as 1893, but she never publicly advocated Zionism until she addressed the Baltimore chapter of the Council of Jewish Women in 1896. In 1907 Rabbi Judah L. Magnes, of Temple Emanuel in New York, invited her to become an honorary member of the Hadassah Study Circle, which, at its inception, was a group of fifteen women who met to study and discuss Judaism and Zionism. Her account to these women of what she saw in Palestine in 1909, says Rose Zeitlin, "brought a new orientation to the group—organization on a national scale, with the specific aim of practical work in Palestine, education in America." At Purim (February 24) in 1912, the Temple Emanuel women turned themselves into the Hadassah Chapter of a nationwide organization to be known as the Daughters of Zion, with the purpose of establishing a public clinic and visiting nurses in Jerusalem, with special emphasis upon the treatment of trachoma in children. As president, Henrietta Szold organized the American Zionist Medical Unit, and in 1918 she became director of the Department of Education. The first two nurses were sent to Jerusalem in 1913; five years later there were forty-four doctors, dentists, nurses, and engineers. Meanwhile, in 1916, Mrs. Szold had died, and Judge Julian W. Mack and others made arrangements to provide her daughter with a stipend, so that she could devote all her time to Zionist work. Between 1920, when she went to Palestine, and 1927, she functioned in various administrative capacities, sometimes with and sometimes without the aid of a medical director, and established numerous health services as well as school playground and luncheon systems, vocational schools, and much besides. She was also involved in causing Mr. and Mrs. Nathan Straus to establish health centers in Jerusalem and Tel Aviv. In 1930, when she was seventy, she received the degree of Doctor of Hebrew Letters from the Jewish Institute of Religion.

She was planning to return to the United States in 1933, but Adolf Hitler ordained otherwise, and she stayed in Palestine to work out a plan originated by Recha Freier, wife of a Berlin rabbi, to save Jewish children by bringing them to Palestine from Germany and other countries menaced by the Nazis, so that the young people could be trained to live and work there; Youth Aliyah was established to perform this function. Henrietta Szold herself visited Berlin in 1933 and subsequently, and in February 1934 the first group arrived. This was a tremendous and a challenging task, enlisting all her devotion, patience, and courage, and it was the crowning achievement of her life. Neither Jews nor non-Jews were of a single mind on the subject of Zionism per se, but no decent human being, whether nationalist or assimilationist, whether he believed in Judaism as a nation or only as a religious community, could deny the importance or the necessity of this life-saving work. The way Hen-

rietta Szold handled it would have been a triumph for anyone; for a woman in her seventies and eighties it came close
to being a miracle. When, at three o'clock in the morning, on
March 13, 1944, she listened over an international radio
hook-up, to her citation at Boston University as "Doctor of
Humanity," which she regarded as the crowning honor of
her life, she was an invalid who had eleven months to the
day left to live. On February 13, 1945, she died in Hadassah Hebrew University Hospital, and the next day she was
buried in the Jewish Cemetery on the Mount of Olives.

II

How was she equipped and prepared for the great work she
did, intellectually, emotionally, and temperamentally? To
begin with, one must say frankly that she wasn't, as she
would have been the first to admit, as she did indeed often
proclaim. She began teaching and writing before she knew
enough to do either, and she died performing herculean
tasks for none of which she had been trained; no woman in
history better illustrates the truth that much of the world's
work has been done by people who did not know enough
and were not strong enough to do it but who went ahead
and did it anyway, simply because it needed to be done.

In her youth she seems to have impressed some observers
as portly, but she grew frailer looking in her later years. Her
sisters considered her a "stick-in-the-mud," "prim and pre-
cise and old-maidish," like a cat in her love of home and her
desire to stay put, which would seem to have been the worst
possible preparation for the life she was to lead. She found
much to admire in the Russian Jews who poured into Baltimore in the 1880s and in the youngsters who came to Palestine in her old age, but both groups repelled her by their
inefficiency and lack of system. She did calisthenics every
morning and showed interest in tightening her stomach
muscles, and if she was proud of anything about her appearance it was her hair and her slim ankles. She brushed her hair
with a hundred strokes every day, and when it seemed to be
growing in again after illness in her old age, she rejoiced because she did not wish to be "a bald-headed old hag." She

never lost her early meticulousness in keeping accounts, and when she was on an expense account and chose to indulge herself at a restaurant in some delicacy she did not think strictly necessary, she always insisted upon two checks, so that she might pay for the luxury herself.

Her capacity for work was phenomenal. Though she never drove her subordinates, she did drive herself far beyond what most of us would have regarded as the breaking point. "Why will you never take a rest?" her sister Rachel once asked her. "You are so sensible and wise in all matters except those which affect yourself directly." We hear of eighteen- and twenty-hour working days. In Jerusalem in 1921 she writes that her day extends from 4:30 in the morning until midnight, and as early as 1891 she declares that "if I wished to do justice to all of the demands made upon me I would not eat dinner except on Friday, Saturday, and Sunday." She horrified Morris Jastrow by advising him to get up and start work at five o'clock, which mere suggestion caused his blood to run cold, his hair to stand on end, and his skin to bristle. In 1931, when she was seventy-one, she began getting to the office at nine instead of seven and leaving "when all other well-regulated humans leave it," devoting the time she had saved to "systematic reading," but in 1937 she still reports that she is working twelve hours a day, and she was eighty-two when she one day interviewed refugee children from eight to three, attended conferences from three to seven, and then, after resting, rose at four A.M. and began a four-hour drive to be on time for an 8:15 meeting. It was fortunate that she felt it a necessary religious duty to rest on the Sabbath; perhaps this may even have prolonged her life.

So, you say, she must have been an exceptionally strong woman, with impregnable health, and the body must indeed have been well enough, since it served her for eighty-five years. Only the uncomfortable question intrudes itself: would the rest of us be able to come closer to hailing distance of her if we cared as much as she did and were capable of similar devotion? Her sister Adele once said that compared to Henrietta even her parents were pagan hedonists. Nobody was in a better position to know than Adele, for when, as a child, she had scarlet fever, Henrietta had herself shut up with her, to nurse her and read to her and humor her, in order to free their mother for other duties. Henrietta had an operation in 1911; in 1922 she complained of the "pathetic little puckers" that had appeared around her lips, her whitened hair, and her impaired hearing, though she still insisted that she did not feel old; in 1944, the year before her death, dysentery, pneumonia, and gout joined forces to lay her low. Overstrained eyes seem to have given her more trouble than her ears, however, and the most serious difficulty was her heart. As early as 1919 she admits she had known for more than three years that it was in bad shape and needed rest, and even after a vacation she finds that she needs twice as much sleep as she used to take, which, to be sure, in her case was not much. In January 1920 she tells Alice Seligsburg that she has aged during the past year and a half and is "physically much less resistant." In the fall her heart acts up again, though she reports with charming vanity that a woman has estimated her age as thirty-eight, so that obviously she is not yet a *"nebbich."* It was a pleasure sometimes to find herself less wearied after an expedition than some of her younger associates. If she would give in to her friends, she knows they would make an old woman of her, "sitting back in an easy chair and letting others do for me," but though she admits she might be old enough for this, she insists she is not meek enough. Even when, in 1938, the doctor told her she had a "tired heart" (actually it was angina) and put her in Hadassah Hospital, she insisted that it was only a heart that had been beating for seventy-eight years.

If she ever had any selfish or personal ambition, it was to become an important writer. The urge to write came while she was very young, as we have seen, and was exercised very freely in the early days, along with her public speaking, which she enjoyed much less. She wrote very well always, with admirable force and clarity, about Jewish writers and heroes of the past and of all the problems that beset her people in the present, never sparing them censure for what she considered their faults. Clearly she found satisfaction in the self-expression her writing afforded her, as distinct from the editorial chores she performed upon the work of others, which was what generally kept her chained to her desk. And from the controversies in which she saw fit to engage, often with people much older than herself, in her *Jewish Messenger* days, it seems clear that she allowed her temperament and even her capacity for indignation to run upon a considerably longer leash when she had a pen in her hand than she did when functioning in her administrative capacities. For she had a temper, and it is important to realize this if only because it makes the control she generally exercised over it all the more remarkable. It was her own view of the matter that she was not "severe" but only "positive, occasionally." Ordinarily an outburst would be triggered by what is generally called righteous indignation, but apparently there were exceptions, for Tamar de Sola Pool records that when she told Henrietta that Mayor LaGuardia was planning to celebrate her seventy-eighth birthday by giving her the freedom of the City of New York, "she flew into one of her extremely rare but famous furious reactions."[5]

In later life Henrietta Szold believed she had "cultivated a scientific detachment," having learned to regard herself "as an object for dissection" while she stood off and watched. Probably no human being has ever really succeeded in doing this, and it may be that those who think they have have succeeded less than others. But there can be no question that she tried, and so seductive is human egotism that, even to the extent that she tried, she was forced to take stock of herself and cultivate interest in her own personality. As we have already seen by reference to her touching response to her honorary degrees, she appreciated recognition from those whose opinions she valued, but she disliked being lionized. "I have never been so heartily tired of anything," she wrote in 1936, "as I have been of myself." Often she thought of herself disparagingly. When, early in life, she met Agnes Repplier, whom she greatly admired, she was sure Miss Repplier must have judged her a very insignificant person, and, like all conscientious people, she had a way of counting and weighing up not her blessings but her failures, real or imaginary. After her sister Sadie died, she reproached herself for not having been sufficiently kind to her, although it is hard to believe this, and, as has already been noted, she felt she had let her father down by not becoming a professional scholar. Theodore Roosevelt always felt that he was not a person of extraordinary capacity and that many average men could have accomplished as much as he did if they had been willing to work as hard at cultivating what they had, and Henrietta Szold seems to have resembled him in this. Probably it never occurred to either that this self-disparagement was, in its way, also a kind of left-handed form of self-praise.

What Henrietta Szold denied especially was unusual intellectual capacity, but she did give herself credit for an "organizing instinct" and a capacity for growth. "I can't understand what is going on around me. . . . I am befuddled by all I read." Yet "while I don't understand, while my intellect is an organ of narrow limitations, my inner world, —perhaps it is my world of feeling, of instinct—expands." She also acknowledged that she possessed a certain warmth of personality, inherited from her father, which she believed drew people to her. "I think people come to me and I warm them up." Certainly she knew that she had done a tremendous job in Palestine and that she had done it well; she would have had to be an idiot not to realize this. "By force of circumstance," she writes, "the Zionists have evolved a medical service which has served, and for some time to come will continue to serve, as a standard to the government itself," and she must have known too that, compared to the maintenance of this work, her personal satisfactions mattered little, even to herself. Her longing to get back to America during her last years was intense and pathetic, but she could not go off and leave her work undone. "The idea of being in America is not a stranger to my mind these days. If I only had a mind, or if I had a mind without a conscience, I'd be there in less time than it takes to say Jack Robinson."

III

But not even so busy and devoted a person as Henrietta Szold can live a life whose energies are completely absorbed by her work (one remembers Emerson's desire to be not a writer but a man writing). What, then, were her other interests, and whence did she draw her strength?

Though she never married, she enjoyed exceptionally close and affectionate relationships within her own family. Irving Fineman does not strain the note when he calls the first main part of his fine biography "Her Father's Daughter" ("So far as I personally am concerned, I am my father's daughter") and the second "Her Mother's Daughter" ("You know my mother, therefore you know me"). Outside the family she did not think she did so well. "I wasted half my life as far as human contacts are concerned," she once said, "because I was bashful. I was in agony." She was far from being a hermit, however. She knew the value of human contacts, and her affectionate nature went out to others. But she was too earnest and sincere a person to find much satisfaction in the meaningless, superficial contacts of what is called "society."

She enjoyed dancing and was light on her feet, and, in her youth, when the Szolds indulged in frequent outings to what was then called "the country," bathing, but there is little indication of any interest in sports or games. When she was a girl, the only game young ladies played outdoors was croquet, and she always "knew enough to run away" from that. On an ocean crossing, however, she was initiated into shuffleboard and discovered to her surprise that she was very good at it. Needlework she enjoyed, but she can hardly have had much time to engage in it.

Her scientific interest was largely confined to botany. She had a passion for flowers and trees. She collected specimens and surrounded herself with growing plants, and when she was homesick in Palestine, it was American forests she missed most, after her family. It was not that she did not respond to the beauty of Palestinian flora. She did, passionately, but she would have liked to have this without giving up what she had left behind. "Rhexis virginica!" she once broke out in a letter to her sister Bertha. "How long since I have either heard the name or seen the flower." Bertha's enumeration of spring blossoms made her "homesick beyond words." And from here she went on to Golden Bantam corn, "fish with flavor, and a walk through ferny woods! It's like hearing the glories of the ancient Temple service and not having the privilege of witnessing them." In Jerusalem too the taste of an apple brought a quick longing for home.

In the early days she came as close to studying plants scientifically as was possible in her environment and with her training. She tried to transplant wild flowers into her back yard and wrote a paper on "Essential Organs of Plants" for the Maryland Academy of Science. She found it impossible to understand how anybody could, as the saying is, love flowers and hate botany. If you liked something, you wanted to know all about it. Could you be fond of a person, she asked, and have no interest in knowing his name?

She was a tireless sightseer, not only in Palestine (where at one time she was more proud of having learned how to ride a donkey, gentle as he was, than of all the work she was doing), but also in Italy, where she was detained on her way to the Middle East, at a time when many people would have been so much annoyed at the disruption of their plans that they would have been in no condition to enjoy anything. "To have to wait in Italy is no mean good fortune," she writes. "And I am trying to get all I can out of it." Even Vesuvius had to be ascended. "These Italian adventures are like drink to a toper." The marvelous paintings in the Italian galleries interested her as much as the landscape. If she had been held up in another country, she says, she could not have stood it, but she underestimates her capacity for adjustment. In Palestine the art was missing, but it was not only the land that enthralled her but the thought of being part of a great pioneering adventure. To be brought face to face with the naked realities that are disguised by the complexities of civilization elsewhere gave new interest to her life. And the tremendous zest, the hunger for life, that she possessed—or was possessed by—must always be kept in mind in trying to understand how she was able to do so much in spite of overwork and illness and discomfort. She could never have accomplished what she did without it. Without it can anyone, one wonders, ever do anything that is worth doing.

But literature and the arts were more important in Henrietta Szold's life than scenery or science or adventure. We hear comparatively little about painting and little or nothing about sculpture until after she got to Europe. She responded warmly to Botticelli, Rembrandt, and Velasquez, and cared much less for Rubens and Veronese, but she never felt that she really appreciated the British painters until she visited the Tate. She greatly enjoyed herself in the Pitti and Uffizi galleries, objecting only (and the objection is itself a touching revelation of her tenderness toward young life) that "Perugino and Fra Filippo Lippi and Botticelli knew how to make fair Madonnas, but not one of them knew what a baby looked like." All their infants had "hydrocephalous heads on grown-up bodies." In Normandy the villages reminded her of Hobbema, Ruysdael, and Paul Potter.

With music she did better—and worse—and again much better. She loved it passionately and was herself enough of a proficient to share in playing Beethoven duets on the piano. There are two rapturous accounts of concerts in Palestine. In one, the Polish violinist Bronislaw Huberman, then nearing the end of his great career, played Bach, Mozart, and Beethoven with indescribable beauty; the other was a program of dance music by composers ranging from Bach to Strauss, played by a string orchestra, under a full moon, in the amphitheater of the Hebrew University of Mount Scopus, which seemed altogether too lovely to coexist in the world with the problems that daily beset her. She could enjoy less lofty music too, and she loved to sing, though she always sang off key, until, at the age of seventy, she made up her mind it was time to correct this and put herself into the hands of a singing teacher who, we are told, took care of the difficulty! In Baltimore the Szolds were a theater-going family also, and perhaps the most daring and picturesque thing Henrietta ever did as a child occurred when the Polish actor Bogumil Dawison came to perform in the German-language theater there and Rabbi Szold, either playfully or seriously, told her he could not afford to buy her a ticket, whereupon she marched off by herself to beard the actor at the Eutaw House, where he was staying, and returned home with two complimentary pasteboards clutched in her little fist.

But literature was more important still. Here Henrietta Szold had a triple heritage. The Bible of course was literature as well as religion, and the culture of the Szolds was almost as much German as Hebrew. Henrietta was reading Goethe's *Hermann und Dorothea* at eight, and when the Hitler menace broke upon the world, she never forgot that he had outraged German culture as well as her own coreligionists. Among the English poets we hear specifically of Wordsworth and Browning (I am surprised to have encountered no reference to Shakespeare), but most of the writers she mentions are novelists. Not all are English. She cared much for *Les Misérables*, and when she read *Thaïs* she wondered if it might have helped her, presumably in connection with her own emotional problems, if she had encountered it earlier. She enjoyed *The Forsyte Saga*, and though she did not find *The Queen's Quair* of Maurice Hewlett a successful novel, she was deeply moved by the portrait of Mary Queen of Scots presented in it. She did not care for Thackeray, but she was enthusiastic about Dickens and George Eliot, the latter especially in *Romola*, which she found "wonderful, psychologically, historically, and artistically." Once, in 1878, she fell asleep over Captain Cuttle in *Dombey and Son*, and being called while he was exhorting her to "hold fast!" and "Stan' by!" cried out, "Where's the steamboat?" and, hastily rising, nearly knocked her head against the door. She read *The Arabian Nights* too, at least in youth, was a charter subscriber to *St. Nicholas*, and never lost her love for *The Wind in the Willows*.

IV

In one of her autobiographical passages, Anne Lindbergh speaks of poetry and music as an unfailing refuge from the sorrows of life. Whatever else fails, she says, these always remain. Long before Anne Lindbergh, Milton had written that "many a man lives a burden to the earth; but a good book is the precious life-blood of a master spirit, embalmed and treasured up on purpose to a life beyond life." Both these statements are true. But most human beings need something else also. And the sources to which they most commonly turn are love and whatever they may know as religion.

As a lover, Henrietta Szold can hardly be called one of the

fortunate ones. Precocious in much else, she was apparently a late bloomer emotionally. She received proposals of marriage both before and after her infatuation with Louis Ginzberg (she might have married Joseph Hertz, who was to become Chief Rabbi of England), but she seems to have given none of them any consideration. As for the Ginzberg affair, it was, on her side, a great classical passion, more intense and more devastating than most persons fortunately ever experience, and it brought her all love's agonies and none of its fulfillment. "I should have had children," she said, "many children," and late in life she added, "I would exchange everything for one child of my own." On this side of the love experience, she did, to be sure, meet with some compensation. When Youth Aliyah got under way, she acquired thousands of children whom she might not have had if she had married, and though they were not children of her body, who could have been more successful in making them children of her spirit? At the end of four years, Youth Aliyah had saved over two thousand; by two years after her death, there were 22,000, and very few had deserted or gone bad. "I have never been concerned with anything in the way of public work," she wrote, "which as impressively as Youth Aliyah made me feel that I am an instrument in the hands of a Higher Power."

If love disappointed her, religion did not. Her own religion, like that of Rebecca Gratz, was as free of fanaticism as of Laodiceanism. Even in her early writings she laments the drift of American Jews away from Judaism, and though she had a high regard for Felix Adler personally, she regarded his adherents in the Ethical Culture Society as "apostates not because new ideas have dawned upon their minds, but because they are swept away by a glittering phrase or a foolish desire to appear fashionable." As we have already seen, both she and her father adhered to conservative Judaism, which saw the necessity to adjust traditionalism to a modern Gentile world yet rejected the reform movement as a kind of pouring out the Jewish baby with the bath, and if Henrietta Szold is ever guilty of intolerance, it must be in her impatience with the reform rabbis who hold their services on Sunday. In Palestine she faced such questions as whether the

boys should be allowed football on the Sabbath (and strad-
dled the fence by deciding that the game might be played as
long as the tickets were purchased beforehand) and the
much more serious question whether it was right to place
refugee Jewish children in homes where Jewish ways were
not observed. But she was always clear that even there to
force a Jew into "the acceptance of a religious form of life"
was "a Hitler attitude." Unless the religious impulse came
from within the heart it was worth nothing, and she was
sometimes sufficiently impatient with the rabbis so that she
confided to a friend, as Rose Zeitlin reports, "that only her
deep religious feeling prevented her from becoming anti-or-
thodox in spirit." Needless to say, however, she never really
did, and nothing shows better how steeped she was in Jewish tradition than the way she was forever conscious of Bib-
lical precedents for everything that was happening today.

Rabbi Szold, who enjoyed cordial relations with Christian clergymen in Baltimore, taught his children familiarity
with the New Testament and introduced them to Christian
services; once, at a ministerial meeting, Cardinal Gibbons
described him as "the best Christian in the room," which
was intended as a generous compliment to him, though it sa-
vors unpleasantly of condescension toward Judaism. As a
child, Henrietta admired the sedately attired and quietly
moving Quaker women of Baltimore for what seemed their
gracious serenity and the atmosphere of peace they exhaled;
later, after she had learned through her own experience
what turmoil and agony can be hidden under a calm exteri-
or, she wondered whether any human being could be quite
so serene as they seemed. I find no indication that she ever
observed Christmas as the atheist Jew Emma Goldman did,
but she certainly respected it for the kindness and humanitarian feeling associated with it; perhaps Dickens had
helped her to see this.

I would consider it almost a sin to say one word against the Christmas festival; it opens so many hearts and tears them out of their
self-absorption; friends are tied closer in the bonds of friendship;
enemies are forgetful of hatred and animosity and join with zest in
the pleasure of the season; the poor are remembered and amply
provided for; not a household but has for its intimates joy and love

on that day. . . . Christmas truly fulfills its mission of bringing peace and good will to men.

In England, cathedrals like York and Lincoln inspired much the same kind of religious feeling in her as they do in Christians, and she quotes Hawthorne, who said that York Minster looked "as though it had dropped from heaven and aspired to return thither," but she admits a pang of jealousy when she compares them to the "loft in a stable-like building" with which the Jewish families of York had to make do. Her reaction to the splendors and luxuries of St. Mark's and other Italian churches was somewhat different, but many Christians have agreed with her in finding more pagan splendor here than anything to suggest either the Christian spirit or its Judaic inheritance.

V

Having tried to probe the spirit of Henrietta Szold from various directions, we may well conclude our examination of her by reference to her relationship to an issue which is still unresolved and which still divides both Jews and Christians. Though she was one of the most ardent and one of the most useful of Zionists, she stood as Zionist with Judah Magnes and Martin Buber and not with David Ben-Gurion and his successors. What she wanted was a homeland where the Jews and their "cousins" the Arabs could live together in peace. In a country so underpopulated, she argued, "the Jews need not and will not rob the handful of Arabs of their rights or their property."

Agree or disagree with this view, the point here is that it is completely consistent with everything else Henrietta Szold believed and an inevitable expression of her personality. She had no sympathy with "national conceit or chauvinism" in any people, and though she certainly believed that her own Jewish birth, faith, and culture imposed upon her the inescapable obligation of loyalty to her people, she did not think them superior to other peoples because she happened to be one of them. When she asks herself, as she often does, "Why are we so hated?" she often adds, "Why are we so hateful?"

and not even Amy Levy could be more merciless in her description of Jewish shortcomings. In Kansas City, in 1917, she writes, "As I go about, I become impressed all over again with the essential worth of the Jewish material, but also with the ugliness with which it is overlaid as by a deposit left by ages of untrueness to self," and in Jerusalem in 1921, "We are raising an arrogant, self-sufficient generation." On balance she believed that "the Jews, whom Jeremiah and myself criticize so unmercifully, are a wonderful people–even the German Jews," but she was also convinced that it would do them no good to gloss over their faults.

Furthermore it must be remembered that Miss Szold was and considered herself a pacifist. In 1915 she rejoiced that the United States was not involved in "the insensate struggle of the Old World." In 1916 she supported Wilson. In March 1917 she laments that America is "being drawn into the bloody maelstrom" and is "heartsick" over the hatred, suspicion, and jealousy that are building up in this country. The following January, she is "in a measure comforted by one of Wilson's messages—"we pacifists have not labored in vain" —and in March she writes a friend that since she is now "ready to fight for the people," though she could not fight for the kings, she is no longer an "orthodox pacifist," though she cannot yet go the length of a Liberty Bond, not approving of "that method of taxation," but in her next letter she admits that she is not happy about all this and that the idea of having somebody else fight and suffer for her is intolerable to her. It soon became clear that the Zionist cause, to which she was committed, was tied up with an Allied victory, yet even before the Balfour Declaration had, as she believed, been betrayed by the British government, she felt that the taint of the sword had poisoned the Jewish position in Palestine and might well undermine it. By 1922 she can declare that "the war has produced only one of the many beneficent results attributed to it by our whatever-is-is-right optimists: a very much larger circle of men and woman than ever before is thinking thoughts that may bear acts in the generations to come," and she adds, "Do not conclude that this result justifies the war in my eyes or even makes the thought of it bearable. As the days of peace multiply I learn to hate its memory more and more." When the Jewish boys who poured into Palestine under Youth Aliyah wished to enlist in the army, she advised against it.

It was a remarkable testimonial to her breadth and charity that a woman who had dedicated her life to the Jewish cause should never have become guilty of separating the Jewish problem from the human problem. When she saw Hitler destroying German culture, it hurt her because this was the culture upon which she had been nurtured. "But," she says, "I believe I should not react otherwise if a culture remote from me, the Italian, the French, had been violated by such brutality. At bottom it is a question of faith in the perfectibility of man. As a Jew, can one afford not to cling to such a faith?" Nor could she think of the sufferings of the German Jews without remembering that Catholics, Protestants, and socialists were suffering with them.

What she wanted was for Christian, Moslem, and Jew to work together in Palestine for the good of all. Jews and Arabs had worked together in the Middle Ages; why could they not do it now? And if the Jews were superior to their Arab neighbors, let them show it by holding themselves to a higher standard of conduct. Granting that they had done much, she still insisted that they had not done enough. What she was asking of them was that they should practice the righteousness and universalism of Israel's great prophets. What less can a Jew ask of a Jew? And does he not betray his heritage if he fails in this? Once she even spells it out, longing "for an Isaiah to show up our littleness and our demoralization." She never spoke harshly of the Arabs, even when Arab boys threw stones after her in the streets. "It is superfluous to speak of what it means to me to hear day after day of the slaughter of innocent, guiltless men—Jews and Arabs alike." If she was ever harsh toward anybody, it was the British, who, as she believed, had "deliberately thwarted every effort made by the Jews to find a method of conciliation between Jew and Arab. . . . I believe there is a solution; and if we cannot find it, then I consider that Zionism has failed utterly."

In 1935 she feared that the new war whose coming she foresaw would destroy all her work in Palestine. But she was a lady who never lacked the necessary courage to face ultimate questions. Suppose it did? Was that the end? "There are Jews who believe that, if this fortress is captured today by our enemy, the whole Jewish people would be so injured by the loss that it could not recover. My personal faith is otherwise. I believe in the strength of the remnant of Israel even if the remnant is small. Only it must be adequate."

In other words, the City of God was not built by human hands, and human hands cannot destroy it. This is the answer to calamity that has been made in every age by those whose faith is centered in something higher than human might. In such utterances Henrietta Szold herself assumes prophetic stature. And if her people as a whole did not rise to prophetic stature with her, she was still, on this point, in good company with Isaiah, Jeremiah, and the rest of the spiritual giants of her people upon whom she had nourished her soul.

Bibliographies and Notes

Rebecca Gratz (1781–1869)

The only book-length biography of Rebecca Gratz is Rollin D. Osterweis, *Rebecca Gratz: A Study in Charm* (Putnam, 1935); see also his sketch in *Notable American Women, 1607–1950*, vol. 2 (Harvard University Press, Belknap Press, 1971). David Philipson's *Letters of Rebecca Gratz* (The Jewish Publication Society of America, 1929) contains her voluminous correspondence with her brother Ben and his family. Unpublished letters are in the possession of the American Jewish Historical Society, on the campus of Brandeis University, Waltham, Massachusetts, and American Jewish Archives, Cincinnati, Ohio. Sarah Anne Mordecai preserved family memories in *Recollections of My Aunt, Rebecca Gratz*, by "One of her Nieces" (Philadelphia, privately printed, 1893). Miriam Biskin's *Pattern for a Heroine* (Union of American Hebrew Congregations, 1967) is a charming, brief novelized biography, tastefully produced. See also the sketch by Jacob R. Marcus in his *The American Jewish Woman: A Documentary History* (Ktav Publishing House, Inc. and American Jewish Archives, 1981). Those who cannot find a copy of Mrs. Mordecai's excessively rare little book will be grateful for Marcus's extracts from it.

1 See William Vincent Byars, "The Gratz Papers," *Publications of the American Jewish Historical Society* 23 (1915): 1–23.

2 So given in printed sources. Sarah Anne Mordecai gives the number of children as seven and their ages as two to twelve.

3 Like many nineteenth-century letter writers, Rebecca Gratz used the ampersand and frequent dashes. I have changed her ampersands to "and"; I have also changed some dashes to commas and omitted others. In one instance I have added an apostrophe to form a possessive, and I have corrected one misspelled word.

4 Joseph R. Rosenbloom, "Rebecca Gratz and the Jewish Sunday School Movement in Philadelphia," *Publications of the American Jewish Historical Society* 48 (1958): 71–77.

5 Gratz Van Rensselaer, "The Original of Rebecca in *Ivanhoe*," *Century* 24 (1882): 679–82; W. S. Crockett, *The Scott Originals* (T. N. Foulis, 1912). Joseph Jacobs makes a careful examination of all the evidence in

"The Original of Scott's Rebecca," *Publications of the American Jewish Historical Society* 22 (1914): 53–60. Jacobs nominates an 1850 article in the *Jewish Record* as the likely source of Van Renssalaer's purported quotation from Scott.

6   Osterweis, *Rebecca Gratz*, pp. 123–24.

7   For the Davidsons, see Carlin T. Kindilien's article on them in *Notable American Women, 1607–1950*, vol. 1, and for Margaret, see Edward Wagenknecht, *Washington Irving: Moderation Preferred* (Oxford University Press, 1961), pp. 131–32.

8   Philipson, *Letters of Rebecca Gratz*, p. 276.

9   See Joseph R. Rosenbloom, "Rebecca Gratz and Henry Clay: An American Jewess Observes a Leader's Drive for the Presidency," *Journal of the Southern Jewish Historical Society*, 1, October 1929, pp. 11–15.

Emma Lazarus (1849–1887)

During her lifetime Emma Lazarus brought out *Poems and Translations Written Between the Ages of Fourteen and Sixteen* (Hurd and Houghton, 1867); *Admetus and Other Poems* (Hurd and Houghton, 1871); *Alide: An Episode of Goethe's Life* (Lippincott, 1874); *The Spagnoletto* (privately printed, 1876); *Poems and Ballads of Heinrich Heine* (B. Worthington, 1881); *Songs of a Semite: The Dance to Death and Other Poems* (The American Hebrew, 1882).

The most comprehensive collection of her poetry is *The Poems of Emma Lazarus*, in two volumes (Houghton Mifflin, 1889), but this is far from complete.

An Epistle to the Hebrews was serialized in the *American Hebrew* in 1882–83 and published as a book by the Federation of American Zionists in 1900.

Morris U. Schappes has edited *Emma Lazarus: Selections from Her Poetry and Prose*, third revised and enlarged edition (Emma Lazarus Federation of Jewish Women's Clubs, 1967). Literature House/Gregg Press reprinted *Songs of a Semite* in 1976.

The Letters of Emma Lazarus, 1865–1885, edited by Morris U. Schappes, was published by the New York Public Library in 1949. *Letters to Emma Lazarus in the Columbia University Library*, edited by Ralph L. Rusk, was published by Columbia University Press in 1939.

There are biographies by H. E. Jacob, *The World of Emma Lazarus* (Schocken Books, 1949) and Eve Merriam, *Emma Lazarus, Woman with a Torch* (Citadel Press, 1956). For Schappes's corrections of Jacob, see his review in *American Literature* 21 (1949–50): 506–7.

The latest book about her and much the most comprehensive study of her work, with an excellent bibliography, is Dan Vogel, *Emma Lazarus* (Twayne, 1980).

The most important articles about her in addition to those mentioned in the notes are Max I. Baym, "A Neglected Translator of Italian Poetry:

Emma Lazarus," *Italica* 21 (1944): 175–85, and "Emma Lazarus's Approach to Renan and her Essay, 'Renan and the Jews,' " *Publications of the American Jewish Historical Society*, no. 37 (1947), pp. 17–29; Albert Mordell, "Some Neglected Phases of Emma Lazarus's Genius," *Jewish Forum* 32 (1949): 181–82, 187, and "Some Final Words on Emma Lazarus," *Publications of the American Jewish Historical Society*, no. 39 (1949–50), pp. 321–27.

Hertha Pauli, "The Statue of Liberty Finds its Poet," *Commentary* 1 (1945–46): 56–64, is an excellent essay. Other appreciative pieces include Katherine Burton, "A Princess in Israel: Emma Lazarus," *Catholic World* 157 (1943): 190–95; Mary M. Cohen, "Emma Lazarus: Woman; Poet; Patriot," *Poet-Lore* 5 (1893): 320–32; Allen Lesser, in *Weave a Wreath of Laurel: The Lives of Four Jewish Contributors to American Civilization* (Coven Press, 1938); Joseph Lyons, "In Two Divided Streams," *Mainstream*, 7, Autumn 1961, pp. 78–85; Edmund Clarence Stedman, in *Genius and Other Essays* (Moffat, Yard, 1911); and Warwick James Price, "Three Forgotten Poetesses," *Forum* 47 (1912): 361–76. See also Louis Harrap's account in his *The Image of the Jew in American Literature* (The Jewish Publication Society of America, 1974) and Samuel J. Hurwitz in *Notable American Women, 1607–1950*, vol. 2 (Harvard University Press, Belknap Press, 1971).

1   Though hardly anybody else has ever rated this novel very highly, Turgenev evidently meant what he said; he mentioned Emma Lazarus to Thomas Wentworth Higginson when the latter visited him.

2   Stedman did his best to make up for Emerson's neglect by including six poems, including three on Jewish themes, in his *American Anthology*, and Charles W. Moulton also gave Emma Lazarus a place in his *Library of Literary Criticism*.

3   "Emerson's Personality," *Century* 24 (1882): 454–56. "The death of Emerson rounds into a perfect orb one of those radiant lives scattered at wide intervals through history, which become the fixed stars of humanity." Within his bounds, he was "one of the most searching, discriminating, fresh, and delicate of critics," and "his praise, when he bestowed it, was royal, almost overpowering the recipient by its poetic hyperbole." The only entries she makes on the debit side are his comparative ignorance of Heine and Swinburne and his failure to appreciate Poe and Shelley. Emerson's influence seems obvious in "Links," the only piece from *Poems and Translations* reprinted in the collected poems:

> The little and the great are joined in one
> By God's great force. The wondrous golden sun
> Is linked unto the glow-worm's tiny spark;
> The eagle soars to heaven in his flight;
> And in those realms of space, all bathed in light,
> Soar none except the eagle and the lark.

See also Max I. Baym, "Emma Lazarus and Emerson," *Publications of the American Jewish Historical Society* 38 (1949): 261–87.

4 Samuel A. Golden, "An Unpublished Emma Lazarus Letter," *Boston Public Library Quarterly* 10 (1958): 54–55.

5 *Lippincott's Magazine* 16 (1875): 175–78.

6 "Tommaso Salvini," *Century* 23 (1881–82): 110–17; "Salvini's 'King Lear,' " ibid. 26 (1883): 88–91; "Barnay as 'Mark Antony,' " ibid., p. 312.

7 *Lippincott's* 18 (1876): 157–58; ibid. 26 (1880): 83.

8 "The Jewish Problem," *Century* 25 (1883): 602–11.

9 Aaron Kramer, "The Link Between Heinrich Heine and Emma Lazarus," *Publications of the American Jewish Historical Society*, no. 45 (1956–57), pp. 248–57, attempts to trace the development of Emma Lazarus's own Jewish consciousness in her changing response to Heine as shown by the poems she chose to translate. He believes that when she speaks of Heine's "fatal and irreconcilable dualism" and the conflict in him between Hellenism and Hebraism, she is dealing with her own problem and that Heine served as a link between her and the Jewish poets of mediaeval Spain. See also Vogel, *Emma Lazarus*, chap. 9.

10 She did not give up her devotion to classicism without a struggle (insofar as she ever did give it up); see Vogel's further discussion of the matter, *Emma Lazarus*, pp. 109–11. What is probably her fullest statement of what she valued in fiction is in her remarks upon Eugene Fromentin's only novel, *Dominique*, *Critic* 1 (1881): 364–65.

11 *Critic* 1 (1881): 164.

12 Since Longfellow anticipated Emerson's "American Scholar" in both his commencement oration on "Our Native Writers" and his article on "The Defence of Poetry" in the *North American Review* for January 1832, this is not strictly accurate. For a somewhat detailed consideration of this matter, see chap. 8, "The Old and the New," in Edward Wagenknecht, *Longfellow: A Full-Length Portrait* (Longmans, Green, 1955). It would be interesting to know whether Emma Lazarus ever learned that Bret Harte was partly of Jewish ancestry.

13 See Vogel, *Emma Lazarus*, chap. 10, for an interesting attempt to trace this development.

14 *Century* 23 (1882): 939–42.

15 "Russian Christianity versus Modern Judaism," *Century* 24 (1882): 48–56.

16 *Lippincott's* 19 (1877): 229–30.

17 *Scribner's Monthly* 16 (1878): 252–56.

18 "New Light on the Religious Development of Emma Lazarus," *Publications of the American Jewish Historical Society*, no. 42 (1952–53): pp. 81–88.

Amy Levy (1861–1889)

Amy Levy published three collections of poems: *Xantippe and Other Verse* (E. Johnson, 1881); *A Minor Poet and Other Verse* (T. Fisher Unwin, 1884); and *A London Plane-Tree and Other Verse* (T. Fisher Unwin, 1889), and three novels: *The Romance of a Shop* (Cupples and Hurd, 1888); *Reuben Sachs, A Sketch* (Macmillan, 1888); and *Miss Meredith* (Hodder and Stoughton, 1889). The AMS Press reprinted *Reuben Sachs* in 1972. An early fairy play, *The Unhappy Princess*, is said to have been privately printed.

During her last few years, Amy Levy was a prolific magazinist, and I have no complete list of her contributions, many of which were unsigned. In addition to the stories and articles mentioned in the text and in the appended notes, see "The Diary of a Plain Girl," *London Society* 44 (1883): 295–304; "Easter-Tide at Tunbridge Wells," *London Society* 47 (1885): 481–83; "Griselda," *Temple Bar* 84 (1888): 65–96; and "A Slip of the Pen," *Temple Bar* 86 (1889): 371–77. *London Society*, to which she contributed a good deal, was subtitled, "An Illustrated Magazine of Light and Amusing Literature," and many of her contributions to such organs express little of her personality. After having received a proposal of marriage, the "Plain Girl" declares, "I am no longer curious as to how people feel in heaven. I know now." And "Griselda" wonders "if a happier woman ever lived. I often marvel at the injustice of Fate which has favored me so unduly."

By all means the most important article about Amy Levy is Beth Zion Lask, "Amy Levy," *Jewish Historical Society of England Transactions* 11 (1924–27): 168–89, which is valuable not only for criticism but for bibliographical information. There is some interesting comment on *Reuben Sachs* by Montague Frank Modder, *The Jew in the Literature of England* (The Jewish Publication Society of America, 1939). See also the references to Amy Levy in S. C. Cronwright-Schreiner, ed., *The Letters of Olive Schreiner, 1876–1920* (Little, Brown, 1924).

1 E. K. Chambers, "Poetry and Pessimism," *Westminster Review* 138 (1892): 366–76. Chambers admitted that Amy Levy's poems "have fascinated me for hours together. Vividly personal as they are, the pent-up sufferings of hundreds of souls throb through them, launching one on wide seas of melancholy speculation." Regarded as literature, "they have a remarkable charm. They possess all the subtle workmanship, the delicacy of finish, the innumerable scholarly touches, which are so characteristic of the minor verse of our day. . . . They are indeed a human document at least as rich with suggestion as the much discussed diary of Marie Bashkirtseff."

2 Harry Quilter, "Amy Levy: A Reminiscence and a Criticism," in his *Preferences in Art, Life, and Literature* (Swan Sonnenschein & Co., 1892).

3 *Woman's World* 3 (1890): 51–52.

4 She left her papers and her copyrights to her friend Clementina Black,

the dedicatee of *A London Plane-Tree*. By her own choice, she became the second Jew and the first Jewish woman to be cremated in England.

5   See also "Cambridge in the Long." Warwick James Price, "Three Forgotten Poetesses," *Forum* 47 (1912): 361–76, makes her a Clapham factory girl; not only is there no confirmation of this elsewhere but it is hopelessly irreconcilable with what we know of her life.

6   *Cambridge Review* 5 (1883–84): 163–64; *Woman's World* 1 (1888): 178–80.

7   Short stories and criticism, published only serially, will engage us later in connection with various points they may help to illuminate.

8   The only suggestion of anything of the kind I have observed anywhere in Amy Levy's writing is in the passage in the *Shop* where she has Gertrude working "like a nigger."

9   Harry Quilter gives an account of Amy Levy's contacts with nature in Cornwall and of her intercourse with a woman who took care of her when she came there after an illness, which incidentally shows that she could charm. "Out of This World," *London Society* 49 (1886): 53–56, is dated from Cornwall. But even here she writes, "Much as I admire the superior peace, simplicity and beauty of a country life, I know that my own place is among the struggling crowd of dwellers in cities" and compares herself to Browning's "icy fish" in "Caliban upon Setebos."

10   Heine's influence upon Amy Levy was considerable from the time of her first published poem, "Ida Grey." Her most interesting comments on him are in "Jewish Humour," *Jewish Chronicle*, n.s. 908, August 20, 1886, pp. 9–10, where she sees him as the typical Jewish humorist. "The poet stretched on his couch of pain; the nation whose shoulders are sore with the yoke of oppression; both can look up with rueful humourous eyes and crack their jests, as it were, in the face of Fortune. . . . True humour, we are told, has its roots in pathos; there is pathos and to spare, we think, in the laughter that comes up from the Paris lodging, or which surges up to us through the barred gates of the Ghetto." But "there is a limit to human power of suffering no less than to human endurance; sensibilities grow blunted and the finer feelings are lost. A tendency to 'debase the currency' by turning everything into a joke, never to take oneself or one's neighbour quite *au sérieux*, is, perhaps, one of the less pleasing results of our long struggle for existence."

11   "The Poetry of Christina Rossetti," *Woman's World* 1 (1888): 178–89; "James Thomson: A Minor Poet," *Cambridge Review* 4 (1882–83): 240–41, 257–58.

12   See "The Jew in Fiction," *Jewish Chronicle*, n.s. 897, June 4, 1886, p. 13; "Jewish Children," ibid., n.s. 919, November 5, 1886, p. 8.

13   For "Wise in her Generation," see *Woman's World* 3 (1890): 20–22; for "Eldorado at Islington," ibid. 2 (1889): 488–89. There are notices of the Beaumont Trust in *Jewish Chronicle*, n.s. 896, May 28, 1886, p. 4, and elsewhere.

14 *Woman's World* 1 (1888): 364–67.

15 "Between Two Stools," *Temple Bar* 69 (1883): 337–50; "Mrs. Pierrepoint," ibid. 59 (1880): 226–36.

16 The *Cambridge Review* found *Reuben Sachs* written in vitriol, but Beth Zion Lask, who regarded Amy Levy as the greatest Jewess England had produced, reminds us that the characters represent "Kensington and Bayswater Jewry, who in their own material success had ceased to care for the spiritual welfare, or even the material welfare, of their less fortunate brethren. It is a matter of the deepest regret that [Amy Levy] did not know that section of Jewry which, despite its worldly poverty, was imbued then as now with the ideals of Judaism that make every thinking Jew proud of his spiritual heritage." To this writer the novel is an important study of "that portion of Anglo-Jewry that had set up Mammon in place of the God of Israel," a prophetic utterance, and "a cry of protest."

17 In view of the alleged connection between Scott's Rebecca and Rebecca Gratz, the following comment by Amy Levy is interesting: "Generally speaking, the race instincts of Rebecca of York are strong, and she is less apt to give her heart to Ivanhoe, the Saxon knight, than might be imagined."

18 *Gentleman's Magazine* 266 (1899): 417–24.

19 *Jewish Chronicle*, n.s. 919, November 5, 1886, p. 8.

20 "The Recent Telepathic Occurrence at the British Museum," *Woman's World* 1 (1888): 31–32. A dying woman reveals the secret of her love for a man who had evidently cared more for her than he had ever admitted even to himself by manifesting to him at his desk in the reading room of the Museum.

21 The three poems quoted from are the dedication to Clementina Black, "Last Words," and "Contradictions." The punctuation at the end of the second line of the second stanza of "Last Words" is the author's; nothing has been omitted.

22 Bradford, *American Portraits, 1875–1900* (Houghton Mifflin, 1922), pp. 56–57.

23 In this connection there is an interesting passage in the poem "Lohengrin." The first part describes the departure of Lohengrin and the reappearance of Elsa's "young, lost brother" as in the opera. Then comes:

> God, we have lost Thee with much questioning.
> In vain we seek Thy trace by sea and land,
> And in Thine empty fanes where no men sing.
> ' What shall we do through all the weary days?
> Thus wail we and lament. Our eyes we raise,
> And, lo, our Brother with an outstretched hand!

Who or what is "our Brother" in the context of the poem? If mankind is indicated and the service of mankind recommended, we have here something pretty close to Comte's religion of humanity which interested George Eliot. I may add that personally I find the most convincing testimony to Amy

Levy's idealism in the one literary article in which I disagree with her radically, her attack on Howells and James in "The New School of American Fiction," *Temple Bar* 70 (1884): 383–89. "Nothing is too trivial, too sordid, or too far-fetched to engage the attention of these 'fine-art' writers." James, she declares, is to Thackeray as Alma Tadema is to Rembrandt. We know Beatrix Esmond better than Isabel Archer and Colonel Esmond better than Ralph Touchett. James "makes us see a great many things, but we should see them better if we could feel them as well," and Howells's books are like photographs: "no artistic hand has grouped the figures, only posed them very stiffly before his lens." The "moral standard" of both writers "is a low one. It is with the selfish record of selfish people that [they] chiefly occupy themselves. There is never a spark of ideality (Mr. James used to give us occasional flashes), the whole thing is of the earth, earthy." They are "terribly finite," without "a touch of the infinite. . . . And in this finiteness lies the germ of decay." How any critic with Amy Levy's intelligence could see no more than this in James and Howells is beyond my understanding. But my point here is that her own high and lofty ideal of what fiction can and should do is equally impressive.

Lillian D. Wald (1867–1940)

Lillian D. Wald herself published two autobiographical works: *The House on Henry Street* (Holt, 1915) and *Windows on Henry Street* (Atlantic-Little, Brown, 1934). Both are largely anecdotal in method and, except by implication, tell much more about her work than herself. R. L. Duffus wrote her biography in *Lillian Wald, Neighbor and Crusader* (Macmillan, 1938). Beryl Epstein's *Lillian Wald: Angel of Henry Street* (Julian Messner, 1948) is a good biography for young readers.

A number of articles by Lillian Wald, mainly in the *Survey*, her usual outlet, are cited in the notes; others may be located through the periodical indexes. The most important articles about her are Paul U. Kellogg, "Settler and Trail-Blazer," *Survey* 57 (1926–27): 777–80; Jerome Beatty, "She Never Gave Up," *Forum* 96 (1936): 70–73; and Helen Huntington Smith, "Rampant but Respectable," *New Yorker*, 5, December 14, 1929, pp. 32–35.

Margaret Wales, *The Public Health Nurse in Action* (Macmillan, 1941) has an introduction by Lillian Wald. Victor Robinson, *White Caps* (Lippincott, 1946) and Edna Yost, *American Women in Nursing* (Lippincott, 1947) are other books in this field which give consideration to her work. More general brief consideration will be found in Adolph Gillis and Roland Ketchum, *Our America* . . . (Little, Brown, 1936); Philip Henry Lotz, ed., *Distinguished American Jews* (Association Press, 1945); and Oscar Handlin, ed., *This Was America* (Harvard University Press, 1949).

1   *Survey* 42 (1919): 595.
2   "Personals," *Survey* 30 (1913): 551–52.

3 George W. Alger, "Lillian D. Wald: The Memories of an Old Friend," *Survey Graphic* 23 (1940): 512–14.

4 *Survey* 45 (1920–21): 4.

5 In her "Female Support and Political Activism: Lillian Wald, Crystal Eastman, Emma Goldman," in *A Heritage of Her Own: Toward a New Social History of American Women*, ed. Nancy F. Cott and Elizabeth H. Fleck (Simon and Schuster, 1979). The writer concludes: "Lillian Wald had structured her life to avoid becoming anybody's possession. When she did get involved in emotional enthusiasms, as soon as the woman involved sought to redirect her priorities Wald's enthusiasm evaporated."

6 *Survey* 68 (1932): 590–91.

7 See Lillian D. Wald, "Public Health in Soviet Russia," *Survey* 53 (1934): 270–74.

8 See her letter, "Helping the Workers," *Outlook and Independent* 156 (1930): 158.

9 See the account of this matter in Duffus, *Lillian Wald*, pp. 155–58.

10 For her most considered comment on anti-Semitism, see "A Social Worker's Viewpoint, *Opinion*, 6, October 1936, pp. 16–17.

Emma Goldman (1869–1940)

The three most indispensable books for the study of Emma Goldman are her autobiography, *Living My Life*; Richard Drinnon's definitive biography, *Rebel in Paradise*; and *Nowhere at Home: Letters from Exile of Emma Goldman and Alexander Berkman*, edited by Richard and Anna Maria Drinnon (Schocken Books, 1975). *Living My Life* was originally published in two volumes by Alfred A. Knopf in 1931, later made available complete in Dover paperbacks. In 1977, New American Library published an abridged paperback edition, with additional material by the Drinnons. *Rebel in Paradise*, originally published by the University of Chicago Press in 1961, was republished by Harper & Row-Colophon in 1976.

Both *Rebel in Paradise* and the New American Library edition of *Living My Life* contain invaluable bibliographical essays which cover many items not mentioned here, including a considerable amount of creative writing inspired by the striking recent revival of interest in Emma Goldman.

Aside from *Living My Life*, the most important of Emma Goldman's own books is *Anarchism and Other Essays*, originally published by her own Mother Earth Publishing Association in 1917 and reprinted by Dover in 1969. It contains much material which originally appeared in *Mother Earth* (whose files, of course, contain much material from her pen which has not been separately reprinted); some of these essays have also appeared in pamphlet form. Alix Kates Shulman's anthology, *Red Emma Speaks: Selected Writings and Speeches of Emma Goldman* (Random House, 1972) covers Emma Goldman's entire career; see also Ms. Shulman's biography, *To the Barricades: The Anarchist Life of Emma Goldman* (Crowell, 1971), as well as Joseph Ishill, *Emma Goldman: A Challenging Social Rebel* (Oriole Press, 1957). Winifred L. Fraser's *E.G. and E.G.O.: Emma Goldman and* The Iceman Cometh (The University Presses of Florida, 1974) is an interesting, inconclusive study of possible influence. Other relevant material is indicated in the following notes and in Drinnon's two bibliographical essays.

1   Now combined with the adjoining Forest Home under the name of the latter.

2   Claire Bloom, *Limelight and After: The Education of an Actress* (Harper & Row, 1982).

3   Though a much less spectacular figure than Emma Goldman, Voltairine de Cleyre is interesting and important in her own right. See Paul Avrich, *An American Anarchist: The Life of Voltairine de Cleyre* (Princeton University Press, 1978), which covers, along with much else, the relations between the two women. Though ideological comrades, they were temperamentally antithetical and never really liked each other. Nevertheless Emma Goldman's *Voltairine de Cleyre* (Oriole Press, 1932) is one of her best pieces of writing, an admiring account of "this most gifted and brilliant anarchist woman America has produced."

4   For the trial and execution of the Chicago anarchists, see Henry David, *The History of the Haymarket Affair* (Farrar and Rinehart, 1936). There are three good books about Altgeld: Waldo R. Browne, *Altgeld of Illinois* (B. W. Huebsch, 1924); Harry Barnard, *"Eagle Forgotten": The Life of John Peter Altgeld* (Bobbs-Merrill, 1938); and Ray Ginger, *Altgeld's America: The Lincoln Ideal versus Changing Realities* (Funk & Wagnalls, 1958). For Howell's connection with the case, see Edward Wagenknecht, *William Dean Howells: The Friendly Eye* (Oxford University Press, 1969), pp. 266–70.

5   Frank Harris, "Emma Goldman, The Famous Anarchist," in his *Contemporary Portraits, Fourth Series* (Brentano's, 1923). This paper is valuable, less for what Harris says than for the extensive quotations from Emma Goldman herself included in it.

6   See S. N. Behrman's delightful account of a childhood memory in his "Double Chocolate with Emma and Sasha," *New Yorker,* 29, January 16, 1954, pp. 24–29.

7   Fredric C. Howe, *The Confessions of a Reformer* (Scribners, 1975) relates how Emma Goldman came to Cleveland when Tom Johnson was mayor, planning to hold a meeting there and virtually challenging opposition. Johnson told her she had the same right to free speech that belonged to everybody else, and she held her meeting without interference or interruption. But the disappearance of opposition had taken the wind completely out of her sails, and Howe leaves the impression that he thought she was a little disappointed. Elsewhere he writes: "She presented her ideas with a brutal frankness and disregard for conventions that suggested the advocacy

of force. . . . She was indifferent to material comfort, generous to the last degree. Tolerant of people, but intolerant of institutions, she denounced the latter unsparingly, and dramatized her own radicalism, partly to secure a hearing, partly because she felt the necessity of becoming a martyr to her beliefs, as were other revolutionists in Russia."

8 The use of the "conspiracy" charge was prompted by the fact that conviction under it could carry a stiffer penalty than mere obstruction. The defendants correctly pointed out that it was ridiculous as applied to them, since their opposition to the war and the draft had been completely open and aboveboard. One of the great cartoons of the period showed the smoke of S. S. *Buford*, on which the pair were deported, blotting out Miss Liberty and her torch.

9 Rebecca West was an honorable, outstanding exception: "Emma Goldman is one of the great people of the world. She is a mountain of integrity." Doubleday, Page accepted the book Emma Goldman called "My Two Years in Russia," omitted the last twelve chapters, and published the rest under the title *My Disillusionment in Russia*, in 1923; this they followed in 1924 with *My Further Disillusionment in Russia*. The Crowell-Apollo edition of *My Disillusionment in Russia* (1970) includes everything.

10 Ordway Tead wrote in the *Yale Review*, n.s. 21 (1931–32): 851: "Wholly irrespective of one's interest in her ideas, no sensitive reader can escape the compulsion of this woman's faith in human liberty and her single-minded devotion to the cause of personal freedom, nor fail to find in this autobiography the mirror of a truly great soul and magnificent personality."

11 Hutchins Hapgood, *A Victorian in the Modern World* (Harcourt, Brace, 1939); Charles A. Madison, *Critics and Crusaders: A Century of Protest* (Holt, 1947); Henry F. May, *The End of American Innocence* (Knopf, 1959). Madison's book contains the best brief account of Emma Goldman's career.

12 See *Nowhere at Home*, p. 71.

13 *The Social Significance of the Modern Drama* (Richard G. Badger, 1914), which Van Wyck Brooks calls "the first book of its kind to appear in English," covers selected plays by Ibsen, Strindberg, Sudermann, Hauptmann, Wedekind, Maeterlinck, Rostand, Brieux, Shaw, Galsworthy, Stanley Houghton, Gilda Sowerby, Yeats, Lennox Robinson, T. G. Murray, Tolstoy, Chekhov, Gorki, and Andreyev. It now seems to us to devote too much of its space to summarizing the content of the plays, but there was more justification for this when it appeared than there would be today.

14 See Nancy F. Cott and Elizabeth M. Fleck, eds., *A Heritage of Her Own: Toward a New Social History of American Women* (Simon and Schuster, 1979), pp. 436–37, for an interesting reference to a woman who developed a "crush" on Emma.

15 Reitman was a complex and amazing man, and Emma Goldman's affair with him was rich in ecstasy and anguish; see Alice Wexler, "Emma

Goldman in Love," *Raritan*, 1, Spring 1982, pp. 116–45, announced as an excerpt from a forthcoming book, *Emma Goldman: A Radical in America*. In "Emma Goldman on Mary Wollstonecraft," *Feminist Studies* 7 (1981): 113–21, Ms. Wexler has published Emma's lecture on Mary Wollstonecraft, whom she greatly admired. The editor believes that "in describing her vision of Wollstonecraft, Goldman also described her vision of herself" and that the lecture indicates that her anarchism "was founded, less on an identification with the masses than on a sense of identity with the great rebels and martyrs of the past."

16   See also in this connection her letter to Dr. Samuel D. Schmalhausen in *Nowhere at Home*, pp. 183–85.

Henrietta Szold (1860–1945)

For the life of Henrietta Szold, see Marvin Lowenthal, *Henrietta Szold: Life and Letters* (The Viking Press, 1942); Elma Ehrlich Levinger, *Fighting Angel: The Story of Henrietta Szold* (Behrman House, 1946); Rose Zeitlin, *Henrietta Szold: Record of a Life* (The Dial Press, 1952); Irving Fineman, *Woman of Valor: The Life of Henrietta Szold, 1860–1945* (Simon and Schuster, 1961). Lowenthal's was the pioneering book, the only one written during the subject's lifetime and which she read. Fineman's is by far the most detailed account of her own experience, but Rose Zeitlin gives the most systematic account of her work in Palestine.

There is much about Henrietta Szold in Alexandra Lee Levin, *The Szolds of Lombard Street, A Philadelphia Family, 1859–1909* (The Jewish Publication Society of America, 1960). Henrietta Szold herself wrote *Recent Jewish Progress in Palestine* (The Jewish Publication Society of America, 1915). See also S. U. Nahon, ed., *Henrietta Szold, 1860–1945: Twenty-five Years After Her Death* (Jerusalem: Executive of the World Zionist Organization, 1970).

1   The name is pronounced "sold," from the German *besoldeter*, and, according to Rose Zeitlin, was assumed by a forebear, Michael Sold, the first Jew in Galicia to hold a government post. When one branch of the family removed to Hungary, "the letter *z* had been introduced into the spelling in order to keep the original pronunciation."

2   See Alexandra Lee Levin, "Henrietta Szold and the Russian Immigrant School," *Maryland Historical Magazine* 57 (1962): 1–15.

3   Henrietta Szold's passion for Louis Ginzberg was first made known in print in 1960 by Bertha Szold Levin's daughter-in-law, Alexandra Lee Levin, in *The Szolds of Lombard Street*. The next year Irving Fineman, who had had access to Henrietta Szold's diary, devoted more than a hundred pages to the story in his *Woman of Valor*. Neither of these writers, however, gave the man's name. This remained for Eli Ginzberg to do in his biog-

raphy of his father, *Keeper of the Law: Louis Ginzberg* (The Jewish Publication Society of America, 1966).

4   Eli Ginzberg, *Keeper of the Law*, pp. 128–29.

5   Tamar de Sola Pool, "Henrietta Szold," in *Three Zionist Rishonim in America* (Brith Rishonim, n.d.).

Index

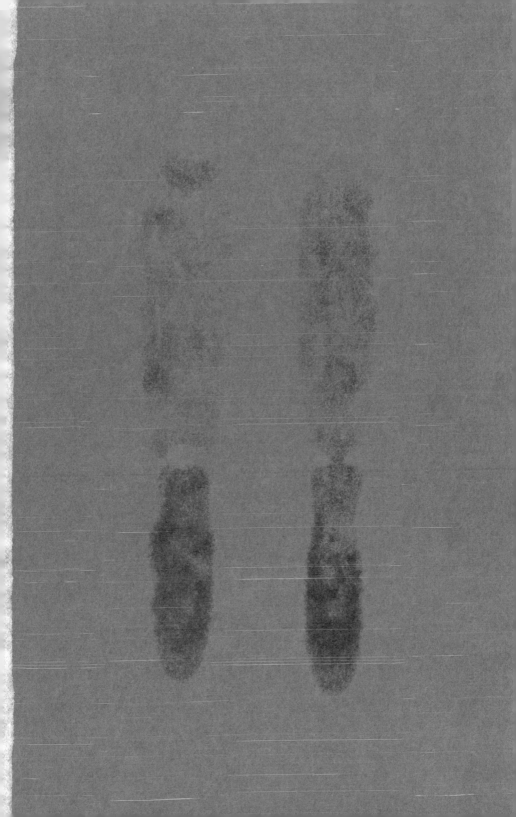

DAUGHTERS OF THE
COVENANT.